Short Stories
from a
Long Career

Short Stories *from a* Long Career

by Virginia F. Lewis

With a Foreword by John Hope Franklin

Progressive Black
Publishing Since 1967

THIRD WORLD PRESS
Chicago

Third World Press
Publishers since 1967

Library of Congress Cataloging-in-Publication Data

Lewis, Virginia, 1907-
   Short stories from a long career / by Virginia Lewis ;
with a foreword by John Hope Franklin.– 1st ed.
      p. cm.
   ISBN 0-88378-266-9 (pbk. edition : alk. paper)
1. Lewis, Virginia, 1907- 2. Teachers–United States–
Biography. 3.   School administrators–United States–
Biography. I. Title.
   LA2317.L57A3 2005
   371.1'0092–dc22

                                        2004025902

First Edition
Printed in the United States of America
Cover design and text layout by Keir Thirus.

Dedication

I dedicate this book, gratefully,

to the many students and teachers who helped to make my career fulfilling and from whom I learned so many valuable lessons for successful teaching and for life;

to my loving parents, Charles W. and Malinda Meaux Lewis, who gave to me the motivation and training to strive in my life to emulate the moral, civic, cultural and spiritual values which their lives so faithfully exemplified;

to the members of my large, extended family (children, grandchildren, godchildren, foster children, nieces and nephews) who have given my husband and me so much love and happiness;

above all

to my beloved husband, Dr. Robert E. Lewis, who for more than seventy-one years was my truly loving companion and best friend, teacher and pupil, classmate and professional colleague, business partner, playmate, aide and encouraging supporter. Sharing everything, joys and sorrows, dreams and successes made our careers and our lives really worthwhile for both of us, and I hope, to some degree for those whose lives we touched.

═══Contents═══

Stories

Thanks

I wish to thank several people whose assistance made this book possible. For valuable suggestions, and for typing, organizing and compilation: Ginger Herring, Valerie Kent Folsom and Richard Folsom. Mary Miller actually found the help I needed and Lovese Purifoy and Louisa Powell typed a portion of the manuscript.

I thank them.

I especially wish to thank the many friends whose comments about my career stories and whose urging finally prompted me to put them in writing, an experience which I found most enjoyable. To my long-time friend, Dr. John Hope Franklin, go my eternal thanks for his assistance with publication.

——Foreword——

Shortly after we moved from New York to Chicago in 1964, Aurelia and I met Bob and Virginia Lewis. They were at the peak of their careers. After long stints of classroom teaching in the Chicago Public Schools, they had moved into administration. He became a district superintendent, and her last position was assistant superintendent of the Chicago Public Schools. They had also reached the pinnacle of training for their professions—both with doctorates in education from Harvard University. I think that we were first drawn to the Lewises because Bob, like Aurelia and me, was a graduate of Fisk; and the alumni from that university know how to appreciate each other. Very shortly, however, our common interests in education and our hope for the rapid advance of all children, especially African American children, bound us together in our efforts to reach a common, distant goal. We admired them greatly.

The Lewises moved away from Chicago to Florida at just about the time we were moving to North Carolina. Our good fortune was that we began to spend a portion of the winter months in St. Petersburg, where Bob and Virginia lived. We were all involved in the Academy of Senior Professionals at Eckerd College. There, our friendship flourished in a way that it did not in Chicago, where we were all too busy to indulge in that luxury. The passing of years gave us a greater appreciation for what the Lewises had done for Chicago and for public education in general.

Virginia and Bob's rich experiences as teachers and administrators did not go unnnoticed or unappreciated in South Florida, as they plunged into the life of Eckerd College and the surrounding area. Soon, they were known and sought after in Tampa, Clearwater, Sarasota, and other cities. They continued to share their rich gifts with their Florida friends and neighbors. Even after Bob passed away, Virginia continued to share her knowledge and wealth of experience with what seemed to be a ever-widening group of friends and admirers.

As a historian, I very much appreciated and valued the perspectives as well as the knowledge and experiences that Virginia Lewis had to offer. Consequently, I nudged her ever so gently to share some of the stories with others who were not so fortunate as those of us who saw her regularly and heard her tell about her rich life. She needed little nudging, for she fully appreciated what her life had been and how it might assist others along the way. I am delighted therefore, that she with the able assistance of Valerie Kent, has been able to share with all of us some vignettes from her wonderful life. And the Third World Press is to be commended for making Virginia Lewis' words of wisdom available to a wider public.

—John Hope Franklin
James B. Duke Professor Emeritus of History at Duke University

Introduction

Virginia Lewis is a national treasure. We are blessed. She should be cloned so that more and more people can be swept into the orbit of her wisdom. Some—most people— just grow old, and Virginia has certainly done that, but with flair. She's 98. A few years beyond the normal span. But many, in fact, most people who grow old, fail to grow wise. Virginia grew wise. And Virginia has changed the world.

She is and has been a teacher all her life. It was her first ambition, and it has been her life's work. She has taken so many little tabula rasa's and has written large upon them. White children, black children, it made no difference; from kindergarten to graduation day, they were all her children. It was her calling to teach them. And even though she's never given birth to a biological child, she is Mother Earth, Gaia, who gives birth and nurtures all her offspring. When they had nothing, she gave them hope because of the gifts she saw and carefully brought to fruition so that they could take their place as the educated citizenry a democracy demands. Her multi-colored and multi-talented children are scattered throughout the world. The seeds she has sown have taken root in many countries, and now her godchildren speak many languages as they carry the messages that she implanted.

I didn't get to really know Virginia until she and her husband, Robert, came to one of my college classes. At the time we were reading Alice Walker's essays, and it struck me that this eighty-something couple had lived through the period that Walker was writing about. I had heard that Robert's father had been a slave. When they agreed to come and speak to my class, little did I know that it would be the beginning of a love affair between my students and this erudite couple, both with Ph.D's from Harvard. Both were teachers, both submerged in the black experience (and it was a black experience in the years before the civil rights act), partners, enlightened rather than embittered by that experience.

Robert died, and Virginia, after 71 years of marriage, had to carry on alone. The classes, and her lifetime commitment to teaching, helped her through that most difficult grieving time. She came to classes alone, and she continued to inspire all who listened to her. She was walking to class at first, then she came in a wheel chair. Now, our class goes to her, and we meet in the Conference Room at College Harbor. My students, in a culture that worships youth, revere this icon of wisdom. How many people at age ninety-eight (that's 98!) can teach a college class? We should clone her.

*****

It was a beautiful Florida afternoon in St. Petersburg when I drove on the Eckerd College campus to College Harbor, where Virginia lives. It seems the perfect spot for her retirement years, because with all those students in close proximity, she has never really retired. They are her extended family. The many flowers on her window sill were thriving, just as her students had done. Life hits the high notes in her presence—even the flowers respond to her aura. Across the room from Virginia with my notepad, we both decided it would be best for her to answer at her own speed and in her own voice. I asked if she would write out her answers to the questions I had. It was a lot to ask, for even though Virginia has a state-of-the-art computer, I knew she wrote mostly by hand. But she agreed. My list of questions was topped by my curiosity about her feelings when working with adult students. Her answers form the mozaic of this piece.

– Valerie Kent Folsom

Learning From The Students

I Can't Do All Of That

One of the first lessons I learned about teaching (a very helpful one) was when I placed an arithmetic exercise on the board for my second grade class at what was then the Washington Elementary School in Chicago. The children had been learning simple addition, so as a practice assignment for half of the class (while I taught reading to the other half), I gave them sixteen problems covering the facts we had been learning by means of oral games, flash cards, etc.

Each child was provided with a sheet of paper and I instructed them and demonstrated how to fold the paper twice vertically and twice horizontally, thereby producing sixteen squares, one for each problem, such as 436 plus 523. The children seemed pleased that they were able to do such "big" problems and not simply 5 plus 4, for example. As they settled to the task, I turned my attention to my reading class.

Perhaps five minutes had passed when I noticed that one little boy was not writing, but crying. I asked, "Sammy, what is the matter?"

He replied, sorrowfully, "I can't do all of that."

Therein was a lesson for me. Sammy was not unwilling; he was simply overwhelmed. For him, it was too much all at once. I said, "Okay, Sammy, see if you can do just the first line and then tiptoe over here and let me see it." His face brightened and he went to work. After the first row was done, I encouraged a smiling Sammy to try the second. He gladly continued to work and finally a beaming face proclaimed that he had accomplished the whole assignment. His ego was uplifted because he learned that he could do a "big job" just like the other boys and girls.

I realized that for some people, tasks may need to be broken into segments, into what seems to be an achievable or possible task. I hope that experience helped Sammy as he faced later challenges. It certainly made me a better teacher. And, at times, later on I was able to help other young teachers whom I supervised.

Just Tell Me What To Do

A similar message came to me after the principal stopped in my sixth grade classroom and asked for a boy to serve as a messenger for her. I selected one boy who was a little older and very eager. The principal had different messages to be delivered to several classroom teachers and she quickly outlined several things for the boy to do. She then smilingly asked, "Now will you do that?"

The boy replied, "Yes, if you just tell me what you want me to do."

Her instructions were too many at once, too detailed, and completely confusing. The boy, like Sammy, was overwhelmed. I intervened and wrote the tasks on a list and handed it to the student. He happily proceeded on his way. This was another helpful experience and lesson for me.

It's Dark Outside

Another lesson came when I walked down the corridor and saw a display of students' art work outside the classroom. One child's work was a piece of paper which he had painted completely black. The art teacher explained that the child had described his painting thus: "It's Halloween night and it's dark outside and can't nobody see nothin'." She added his "story" just below his picture. To him (and then to others), the picture had meaning. She was a wise teacher not to reject his painting because she didn't understand it, but to wait for his interpretation and to display it with the others. Each child in her class was thus rewarded and motivated.

Maybe We Were Crying

One incident that made me a more understanding teacher occurred many years later. I had recently become the principal of a large Chicago high school, Wendell Phillips. I was fortunate to have Mrs. Wirth, a teacher in our English department, who taught Drama. She was so talented that the students produced plays worthy of the professional theatrical stage. We were very proud of their performances.

On one occasion, the play was *Little Women.* Our very large auditorium was filled with the teen-age students. The play had reached a scene which was very sad and it was being performed exceedingly well. To my surprise, at this sad moment in the play, I heard giggles and subdued laughter from the audience. I was startled, then greatly annoyed. I stopped the play for a few minutes. Then I asked, "Are you ready to resume as a respectful audience?" The students, well aware of my displeasure, were thereafter quiet, orderly, and attentive throughout the remainder of the program.

What was the lesson I learned? A short time later, when she caught me alone, one of the students said to me, "Mrs. Lewis, did it occur to you that we might be laughing to keep from crying?" No, it hadn't occurred to me, but her question brought realization. I realized that these were not mature adults; these were teenagers. They were growing through a period when they were probably just learning to handle their emotions. In addition, I remembered how they might hesitate to let their fellow classmates see them crying lest they be considered weak or infantile.

Understanding my teenage pupils better was a great help to me in many situations as I enjoyed (yes, enjoyed) my ten years as principal of that high school.

Perhaps Some Child Will Share A Lunch

One occurrence brought me real sadness and an awakening to the unfortunate conditions under which some pupils lived. The Montefiore school building (a branch of Washington Elementary School) to which I was first assigned as a teacher had no lunchroom; most of the children went home at noon and returned at 1:15. A few students brought their lunches and ate in the large basement "playroom" located near the washrooms and where recess was held on rainy days.

One day, when I saw her heading for the basement playroom, I asked a pretty little girl in my third grade class if she had brought her lunch. She explained to me that she had not brought lunch because there was no food left in their house. Her mother had told her to go to the basement area where some children would be eating and perhaps some child or children would share their lunch and give her something to eat. She told this to me in a simple, matter-of-fact manner with no special appeal for sympathy. I was horrified. From my own and other teacher's lunches, we could easily provide a lunch for her but the questions that troubled us were whether this had happened before to this or some other child without our knowledge and what could we do to be sure it never happened again. To this day, I recall that revelation as a most painful experience and one which created in me a new awareness of some of the needs and problems which our students may be facing every day.

We Can't Sing That Song

I recall that once during my early teaching days, my young class gave me a surprise. The students were eighty percent Italian, twenty percent Greek, Polish, and of other ancestry. Nearly all of these families were Catholic. I had placed a song on the blackboard, and the pupils had learned it very well so we would be ready to present it at the monthly primary grades assembly. On this day, I said, "Well, children, let's practice our new song." I stood in front of the class, used my pitch pipe to give them the starting note and started to lead the song. There was not a sound; the boys and girls were attentive, but silent. I said, "Perhaps you didn't understand; we will sing our new song." Again, I gave the first note and started to lead. Again, there were solemn faces, but not a note of music. Very much puzzled, I asked, "Children, what is wrong?" One little girl raised her hand and volunteered in an apologetic tone this explanation: "Mary (a class member) was passing the Protestant Church yesterday and they were singing that song, so we can't sing it." Solemn little faces nodded as they looked at me thinking that I would understand. Mary assured me that the story was true.

I silently deplored the fact that these dear little children were being indoctrinated with a religious bigotry;

but, of course, they were in no way to blame. It was not really a religious song, but perhaps they were singing it at that church.

I told the children that I did not think that others singing the song was important, but since they had learned that one so quickly and so well, we could probably do another one. They gladly learned the new song, which I placed on the board the next day. I could tackle bigotry later and without censure of the children.

Relationships With Students

Football Injury

Our students made us very proud of them. It is rewarding to see them learn and achieve success and make their own contributions to society. That's what makes teaching worthwhile to the teacher as well as to the student and to society. I realized that as principal I did identify very closely with the efforts of the students. For example, I did not confess at the time, but I never really could enjoy our school's football games. For the team's sake, I hoped they would win, but it wasn't losing that bothered me. It was the fear that one of the boys would get hurt. I was always relieved when the game was over.

I tried to make an effort to attend as many games as I could; however, I did not attend one particular game because I was not feeling well. It just so happened that during this football game a boy was hurt and taken to the hospital. I received a phone call at my home from the injured boy's brother. He was at the hospital and somewhat distressed. He said the hospital would not admit his brother until they had some assurance that they would be paid. Their mother was not at home and their father, who had the boys insured through his place of employment, could not be reached by telephone. So—the brother called me!

I was upset about the student's injury and furious that a hospital would refuse him even first aid; but I was really happy that his brother had called me. It was rewarding to me that I was "third," after only his mother and father, that he felt free to call me and thought that I would be there ready and willing to help them. I hoped all of my students felt that way.

Of course, I called the hospital, gave them my credentials and assured them of payment and demanded that the boy be given medical attention immediately. Fortunately, it was not too serious an injury.

They Have Your Number

I was, however, curious about one thing. So when the brother called back as I had requested, I had a question for him. First, I thanked him for calling me and complimented him on his good judgment. Then I asked, "But how did you get my phone number? Only my husband's name is listed in the telephone directory."

"Oh," responded the lad, "Mrs. Lewis, all the kids have your phone number." I was astounded because I had never received a call at home from a student or parent and had never been annoyed by problem calls. This gave me another reason to be proud of our Phillips' students and our relationship.

You Made It

Years later, one former student was telling friends how much it meant to him when he approached me on the stage to receive his diploma and I said softly to him, "You made it." This was a lad who had been in trouble several times and was about to be transferred from our school. I had heard his plea for another chance and his promise to make good, and I had given him that chance. He had kept his promise and he was glad to find that I remembered when I gave him those special words of congratulation.

Is He Going Your Way?

A somewhat amusing incident was repeated several times. A girl student would confide happily, "Mrs. Lewis, I have a new boy friend," and my reply was usually, "Good. Would I like him?" If the girl agreed readily, my next question would be, "Is he going your way?" She understood that to mean whether he had goals similar to hers, whether she would be proud, later, to be identified with him and have children just like him.

If the girl, however, hesitated to answer my first question readily and affirmatively, I would say at once that her uncertainty indicated that there was something wrong and I did not hesitate to warn her to go very slowly with this new friendship where she already suspected that, as a person or a student, his behavior—his lifestyle, his code of ethics, his goals, etcetera—left something to be desired.

You Saved My Life

One former student, who became a fine teacher and later a college professor, surprised me by saying, "You saved my life." She said that she had been a "terror" in grammar school and was starting on a wrong path in high school, but was soon jolted into a realization of what was going to be required of her. An especially intelligent girl with a great talent for leadership, she soon became an asset to our student body and a joy to her teachers.

Another former student used the same words to describe how she was given a second chance and, living up to her promise, had restructured her life and become, herself, a successful educator.

Farewell to Phillips

When I was leaving Phillips High School to become the Superintendent of District Twenty, there was a farewell assembly. The school choir sang beautifully and the program enabled me to give a parting "blessing." We tried to hide the tears. The school newspaper, however, had an article about my departure and the title was something I have always remembered and cherished. It said, "We Have Lost Our Beloved." That was ample repayment for the ten years devoted to those students.

It was some comfort in later years to have my beloved school in good hands; first my husband, Dr. Robert Lewis, and then our capable colleague, Dr. Alonzo Crim, became the principal.

Pride In Students

Breathe

One incident revealed the depth of my involvement with my students. In retrospect I had to laugh at myself. Our choir was participating in the annual city-wide contest among high schools to see which choirs could obtain an evaluation of "Superior." This was a coveted rating and our choir had been preparing for the event.

I was in the audience, of course, and when it was our choir's turn to take the stage, I guess I was like a proud mother. At any rate, as they were singing beautifully, I suddenly felt faint and I realized that I was holding my breath. I was so involved in their performance that I actually was not breathing and was nearing a blackout. Of course, I was okay after a few deep breaths, and I was careful until they left the stage. (Yes, they did earn the "Superior" rating).

Celebrities

We were fortunate, through the kindness of the manager of the Woods theater and other friends, to be able to bring to our school famous people from stage and screen careers. The young people were thrilled to have Harry Belafonte, Sidney Poitier, Lena Horne, opera star Winters and others. Our program of inspiration and motivation also included less famous individuals, like former students who were achieving and making worthwhile contributions to our society and even our neighborhood. We had businessmen, local storekeepers, other successful tradesmen, and other professionals to visit our high school.

It was the students' questions to the celebrities that were especially rewarding. Of course, some did ask about life in Hollywood and probed for details of celebrity life. But for the most part, the students wanted to know how these individuals were able to succeed—what steps they took, when they began, who helped them or what obstacles they had to overcome and how this was done. There was always an in-depth interplay with each of these famous guests and others. The students were encouraged and really thrilled and so were members of the faculty lucky enough to be in attendance at those auditorium sessions. We had great role models from far and near.

A Teacher's Reward

I remember an inspiring day when I participated in the oral examinations for prospective teachers. A young lady who had been substituting briefly in the schools was asked to relate some happy teaching experience. She told us that she had been given a first-grade class of new pupils. One of her activities was to print a story on the blackboard, a story she copied from the book the children would use later. She told the story to the children and then read it from the board. She encouraged them to join her in reading it over and over. She then produced flash cards containing words in the story. The children played many games with these cards, first matching them to words on the board, then just telling what each card said as they flashed them to one another.

When she was assured by these games, interspersed through the day, that the children knew all of the words, she prepared a surprise. When the children returned from their recess period, each one found a pretty book on the desk. Wondering and curious, they opened their books and found a picture of the dog in the story and words which they knew on the pages. One little girl was so excited with her discovery that she ran from her seat to the teacher, waving the book in her hand as she cried out, "I can read! I can read!" The joy in that one child's face was enough to thrill the young teacher. She experienced, she said, the satisfaction and great reward that comes to a teacher. The other students were also happy and the teacher let them read to her, different pupils sharing parts of the story. They were permitted to take their books home overnight to show their families, and the teacher printed a new story on the blackboard for the next day, using many of the same words. The second book, likewise built on those stories, gradually introduced new words. The teacher said she was "hooked for life" into a teaching career and her students were eager for reading lessons.

Modern Dance

One incident which filled me with pride in our children was when we had visitors from another school (several teachers) to see if we could plan some activity to bring our students together. Our students were all black and the other students were all white. We were seated in the conference room and the Physical Education teacher had brought in a few students from our Modern Dance Class to meet our guests and make plans. The visitors seemed pleased, and one of them asked eagerly if the students could dance for her. We agreed, but then she asked for a particular dance (something, I learned later, which was new and especially sexy).

Before the dance instructor could respond, one of the dancers spoke in a very scornful tone saying, "Oh no. We don't do that kind of dancing. We show motion, but we don't just shake." Her teacher and I were speechless, but proud; and, as the girls performed for us, I was even more pleased. It was like seeing part of a ballet, graceful and classical. Our guests were surely surprised and gave evidence of their appreciation.

Satisfaction

Other sources of satisfaction have been the success stories of former students who are now making significant contributions to society. Graduates of Phillips High School have an organization, which receives nominations and selects individuals for the "Roll of Honor", which hangs their pictures in the school hall and also provides scholarships to graduates. I get letters (and some calls and visits) to me which say: "You saved my life." "You made it happen." "I want you to know that I am trying." I even received letters from teachers who have continued their education: "You were my role model." These are some of the rewards of a teaching career.

One former student, Carl Boyd, has written a book dedicated to my husband and me! *The Last of the Old School Educators,* in which many students credit us with influencing their lives in a positive way.

Boundaries

Three Gold Stars

I wish I could tell the full stories of three cases for which I felt I had obtained a "gold star," but details might make the persons involved identifiable, so I can only mention the incidents.

On one occasion, I discovered that one of my splendid male teachers was becoming "too involved" with a student aide in our high school. She was helping him after school each day checking books and doing other chores. Her relatives were concerned that she was spending an unusual amount of time in his classroom. Alerted, he recognized the danger and made a change. I felt that my intercession may have saved a teacher and a child.

In the other cases, marriages were threatened and probably saved. I refused a staff member's request that we hire, in our office, an alluring female temporary employee. He was obviously attracted to her: taking her to lunch, driving her home each day, etc. Similarly, I refused in a third case to allow a female other than his wife to participate in our out-of-town group activities with him. Without anyone else's knowledge, my refusals resulted in termination of the temptations and two long, and apparently successful marriages, resulted. A principal, I had learned, is still a teacher and the welfare of her charges (teachers, too) is of great concern.

The "Prom"

On two other occasions, I felt it necessary to take action where the teacher had made an unwise and unacceptable choice. I can't recall how I learned that the young physical education teacher, new to our faculty, had been invited by a senior boy to be his "date" for the Senior Prom; and she had accepted. I asked her to meet with me in my office. I am not sure if she knew the reason for my request, so I told her what I had learned, and that I needed to discuss this with her.

Her attitude was a surprise. She didn't see what the problem was. I tried to explain why a teacher could not "date" a student, but she was resentful, indicating that she felt that she and she alone should decide whom she could "date." I finally had to tell her that she could indeed make the decision, but that I would not be able to keep her as a member of our faculty. She was courteous, throughout, and so was I. I may have even seemed maternal and abridging her rights as an adult.

The next day, I received a message that she had cancelled her prom engagement and appreciated my advice and was glad to be able to teach at our high school. I must add that she remained and was a very satisfactory teacher.

Another Skirt

As the District Superintendent, I was visiting one of my schools. It was early morning and the pupils were entering from the playground, led by their classroom teachers.

As this young teacher brought her children down the first floor corridor to their classroom, other pupils were going up the stairs. These were the older students, some of them eighth grade boys. They let out some whistles and "oohs" toward the young teacher. I heard this as I entered the hall, and as they disappeared up the stairs I saw immediately what caused their actions: the teacher was wearing a very tight, form-fitting skirt, which was very short—too short—and too form-fitting. The principal indicated that this young lady sometimes dressed in this manner.

I decided to visit her classroom. She was seated at her desk taking attendance, and when the "tardy bell" rang, one little girl rose, took the flag to the front of the room and said, "Stand." Another little girl took a place beside her and directed the children in singing "The Star Spangled Banner."

I had to give the teacher a sincere compliment on her class organization and control. Then I asked, softly, "But do you have another skirt at home?" Surprised, but chagrined, she replied, also softly, "Yes, I do." I told her the reason for my question: The boys had thought it okay to whistle and make lewd, discourteous calls to her. I said, "You are a beautiful young lady, with what seems to be the promise of being a great teacher, and you deserve better than that; but those short, tight, sexy clothes will get disrespect on the street and even here at school." Her response was a warm smile, a hand shake and a sincere thank you.

Meet Me In The Washroom

A mother and father brought their son, one of our pupils, to my office one morning for a conference. The boy had reported to them that an unmarried male teacher had invited him to meet the teacher in the male teachers' washroom on the first floor. The parents informed me that they were going to the Board of Education to demand the teacher's dismissal. I asked them to wait while I spoke to the teacher and investigated. I did not express belief or disbelief of the boy's story, for I knew that protecting our students from such experiences was a priority.

I was also aware that all accusations are not true and that an angry or failed student sometimes may manufacture a story to "punish" the teacher. If the story was true, it was a terrible action and all of our school, students, and especially our male teachers would suffer from the publicity when the offending teacher was brought before the Board of Education, pending dismissal if he was proved to be guilty.

I summoned the teacher and informed him of the charge. He strongly denied any guilt. He said, however, that he had taught for many years and had a clean record which he would like to maintain and that he would hate to have this charge on his record. He added that he had just buried his mother who left him well off financially. He no longer needed to work and this would be a perfect time for him to resign, which he proceeded to do.

I was able to report to the parents the result of that conference. I was also able to compliment them on their immediate attention to their child's report and to compliment the boy on going at once to his parents for help and advice. There was no publicity; the parents were satisfied that the teacher would not be able to approach their son or any other child.

I was pleased to have this unfortunate case closed so quickly and permanently. It may have been a year later when I read in the newspaper that this teacher was killed in some disagreement among a group of men residing together on the near north side of town.

I took some comfort in the fact that this boy had gone immediately to his "homeroom" teacher with his story. It was she who advised him to tell his parents and have them come to the school and consult me about the situation. I thought that this said something positive about good relationships between some students and their teachers. No matter how delicate the problem, even advances by a teacher, the students could feel confident that his or her "homeroom" teacher would understand and help them.

It indicated something positive about this teacher's relationship to her students. She always attended when the choir was performing somewhere, when there was a dramatic production, or a football or basketball game or whatever involved our students.

She Doesn't Care

I was taking several of our high school cheerleaders somewhere in my car. I was busy driving and they were chattering among themselves. One girl said something about her activities on the previous Saturday night. One of the other girls expressed surprise and asked, "Does your mother let you go there? My mother won't let me go near there."

To which the first girl responded in a most sorrowful tone, "Oh, she doesn't care what I do."

"Oh, that's awful," another girl said sympathetically. It sounded as if the first girl did not feel that she had a mother who cared enough about her to restrict her activities, whatever they were, and the other girl felt that she needed sympathy.

I was glad that they felt comfortable enough to share their feelings in my presence, but I knew it was unnecessary for me to chime in. They obviously had a handle on the situation. A quick change of subject followed when I called out "Girls, we're almost there. Are you ready?"

You Are The Grown-Up

All children desire order and discipline in their lives; and doing what you should do to carry out your responsibility "kindly and firmly" earns respect. I learned this lesson outside of the classroom. My husband and I had taken our granddaughter, Beth, to Hawaii. In the hotel the first evening, for some reason, the child did not want to go to the dining room for dinner. My husband was persuaded to go while I stayed with our granddaughter, being fearful that she was really not well, as she claimed. After a while Beth said, "Grampie has to eat all alone, doesn't he?" And, I replied, "That's your fault; you didn't want to go."

The reply of that seven-year old child was a lesson to be remembered. She said, "Well, you are the grown-up. Why didn't you make me?" I could only reply, "You are right. That was my responsibility. I am sorry, but I will do it now. Put on your shoes and we will join Grampie at dinner." A happy little girl, apparently feeling quite well, went with me to the dining room, and all was well.

Try Me

When I was principal of the high school, a small incident occurred when I was walking in the corridor and heard some noise in the boys' washroom. I knocked on the door and asked the boy who responded to tell the other boys to come out. His hesitance impelled me to add, "If they aren't out here immediately, I'm coming in."

I well remember the shocked, horrified look on his face as he exclaimed, "Ms. Lewis, you wouldn't."

My response was, "Try me." He disappeared and in a few seconds the four boys were lined up before me.

I said, "The tardy bell has rung and you are late. Get into your classes at once." Greatly relieved, I am sure, they sped away. I had no need to be more severe; they would have to make peace with their teachers for being late. Enough! "Don't beat a dead horse."

Teachers Have Tempers Too

Temper!

When I was a very young teacher, one incident not only revealed something to me about myself, but also caused an older and wiser teacher to give me great advice which I was later able to pass on to other young teachers.

I had distributed paper for a lesson and I told the children to take their pencils and begin. To my great surprise one of my little second grade boys immediately broke his pencil in half and threw it on the floor. I said, "Pick up your pencil, Johnny." He responded by taking his twelve-inch ruler, breaking it in half and throwing it, also, on the floor.

I said, "Johnny, you may go into the dressing room," which was an open passageway where coats were hung. Of course, the boy did not move, so I approached his desk and, being bigger and stronger than he, I dragged him out of his seat and marched him into the dressing room. I returned and attempted to resume my lesson with the rest of the class.

It was difficult, however, because Johnny began screaming as loud as possible. I told him to stop the noise, but he continued. At that moment, the principal, who had been passing our classroom, opened the door, looked in the dressing room and said, "Boy, stop that noise." Johnny stopped immediately and the principal left. When he heard the door close, Johnny started screaming again and I remember thinking, "He stopped for him, but not for me."

I had never been a person with a quick temper. Perhaps it was because my mother had taught us, "Temper is a luxury which you cannot afford." But on that morning, I was infuriated. I dashed into the dressing room and told the boy that if he didn't stop, I would throw him to the floor and stamp him through it.

It is amazing what ridiculous things we will do and say if anger takes control of our thoughts and actions. My fury, however, frightened Johnny and he was quiet as I marched him back to his seat, gave him a pencil and proceeded to conduct the class as I had planned. Johnny's family, though new to our school area, soon moved to some other neighborhood and another new school district. But, for the rest of his time with me he was angelic.

Warning

After that incident, an older, wiser teacher indicated that I was very lucky because I had made an error which could have had unpleasant results. She advised me that when a child is misbehaving in my presence, it is dangerous to put him out of my presence. To explain, she told me a story about a little girl whose mother put her in the closet as a punishment. When the mother went to check on the child, she found her puckering her lips in a strange manner. Upon questioning the child she got this reply, "I 'pit on your hat, I 'pit on your coat and now I'm making more 'pit."

I was lucky; Johnny only screamed and didn't harm the garments in the dressing room. In later years, as principal, my teachers always kept misbehavers in sight because of my warning and because of the lesson I learned as a young teacher.

Self-Control

Only one other time did I almost succumb to anger. A boy in my sixth grade class had been misbehaving in some manner and I, still a young teacher, had sent (or taken) him to the principal's office. A short while later he was allowed to return to the classroom. I expected to welcome a subdued, penitent child and so I nodded to him to take his seat. In a few minutes, he removed his large geography book and began slamming it against the desk. Speaking to him was of no avail and conducting the class was impossible. I literally yanked him from his seat, dragged him into the corridor, and down the stairs to the front office. Seeing the principal there, I shoved the boy into the office and left. I felt that on the previous visit the principal had merely told the child to go back and "be a good boy."

I realized, again, the danger of losing one's temper. I could have hurt the child or could have had an accident on the stairs! The principal placed the boy in another classroom and we never discussed the incident. I was reminded that there were better ways of controlling one's classroom than becoming angry. Self-control is imperative for the classroom teacher and for parents as well.

My Mother's "Look"

It is interesting to note, also, that the next day, another little boy broke his pencil and threw it on the floor. In his case, I only had to approach his desk and look directly at him and point to the pencil on the floor to get a meek compliance. I was not angry in this case and was in full control of my feelings, words and actions.

I had realized, after the incident the day before, that I was vulnerable, that I could lose my temper, and that I could wreck the career which I had worked so hard to achieve. So I deliberately used the technique my own mother had used during my childhood. As far back as I can recall, neither of my parents ever slapped or spanked me and I as a teacher never struck a child as a form of discipline. My mother would look at me and that was sufficient even though I really wasn't afraid of her or of my father. I knew that I was much loved (although there was not a lot of caressing) and I didn't want to disappoint them or risk their displeasure or unhappiness. I knew that they had high expectations of me and believed in me. So I used mother's "look" with this second little boy and many times later when my pupils needed a warning or a reprimand.

Using The "Look"

Speaking of using a significant "look" to control a discipline problem reminds me of an experience (which may have been repeated any September when approximately one-fourth of our students were freshmen and new to our school standards of behavior). Seated on the stage of our auditorium, facing more than 1,000 students (about one-half to one-third of our enrollment at various times), I usually was wearing my glasses.

If I heard a sound from any of the students during the program, I made a great display of changing my position (sitting erect), of removing my glasses for a better view of the audience and staring directly at the area from which I had heard talking or whatever. Since my actions were in plain view of everyone, the disturbance, however slight, was immediately discontinued. I then silently replaced my glasses, resumed my relaxed position and gave attention (as did everyone) to the program.

The other aspect of this "performance" on my part causes me, in retrospect, to smile. On another occasion, when I saw or heard "inattention" to the program, I happened not to be wearing my glasses. In that instance, I took my glasses from my lap (or purse) and ceremoniously placed them so I could again get a better view of the audience and the disturbance. The result was the same: immediate silence and attention to the program.

If It Doesn't Work

I am reminded of one incident where my "look" did not work. When a group seemed to continue to have some disorder, I rose, delayed the program regretfully, requested that the division teacher escort the members of her "home room" back to their room because, I explained, "They do not seem to be ready to participate in this kind of assembly." An embarrassed teacher and her approximately 35 embarrassed students marched out of the auditorium and we returned to our program. (It is of interest that such a measure was never necessary again.)

A Bunch Of Keys

A mother and father came to me one morning to complain that the teacher had thrown a bunch of keys and one key had made a small bruise on their son's cheek. It was hard to believe, but true; while they waited, I checked with the teacher. He was so remorseful that I thought he and the parents should meet. I talked to the teacher first, very bluntly and harshly, giving him no support for what I described as stupid, dangerous, and totally unacceptable. Returning to the parents, I agreed on the magnitude of such an act and took their side in condemning the action. I took a little more time, however, to explain what had happened.

The teacher had about 60 students in a choral group. For some reason, the usually well-behaved group was inattentive, even somewhat disorderly. The teacher had struggled with this problem for quite some time but it got no better. Completely frustrated, he lost self-control, tossed his keys away toward the class (not at any one student), and I believe, walked out. Unfortunately, the keys did strike their son. "But," I asked, "How many children do you have? Do they ever try you so much that you lose your temper? And say or do something that you would not have said in a cooler frame of mind? What if you had 60 of them and were responsible for teaching them?" To their understanding nods, I added that the teacher was known to be a fantastic, talented teacher, greatly concerned about his students and that I believed he had learned a lesson about self-control. He was shocked, ashamed and remorseful, I told them.

"Yes," they replied to my question, they would like to meet him. It was a good meeting and both teacher and parents left feeling better. And, so did I.

Old School Discipline

School Pride
And Requirements

We had read in the newspapers about unruly students from another high school who had badly damaged the bus taking them home from a football game. At an assembly before our next game, I asked the students to wear our school colors, blue and white, so that they could be easily identified. I did not want them, I explained, to be confused with other students who might be disorderly. I expressed my confidence in their behavior.

They knew, from previous discussions, that the newspapers would not headline a disorderly "Joe Brown," or "Jim Smith," because few people in the city would know them. The headlines would scream, "Phillips High Students Destroy Bus" or whatever, and all of us would be ashamed. They also knew that such an incident involving our students would mean a cancellation of all games for the rest of the season.

In those days, principals had the authority to make such decisions for the school; therefore, I could take a positive approach, building school pride and a generally understood appreciation of their school and of themselves as a part of it.

A Negative Incident

Surprisingly, we only had one negative incident with unruly students at our school in my ten years as principal. This particular incident involved the freshmen on the wrestling team. They went to Evanston, Illinois for a match and traveled on the elevated train. The next day, we received a report that some of the students returning from their match had, upon entering the train station, grabbed handfuls of candy as they passed the counter and rushed from the station. I was greatly upset because we had built a fine reputation at Phillips and were proud of it.

We called the team together the next day realizing that not all of them were guilty; but having no idea of how many or which ones were responsible, I asked the boys who were guilty to raise their hands so the whole team would not have to suffer. There was no response whatever. Asking the boys to "snitch" on each other was to them unthinkable. I explained to these freshmen the seriousness of the situation and that they would certainly have to reimburse the vendor for the stolen candies. He claimed to have lost $25.00 in merchandise. The boys spoke up for the first time to declare that the value was not nearly $25.00. I explained that we were lucky because since we had no proof of what we took, he could have set the value much higher had he chosen to do so. Therefore, I would expect them to have on my desk by ten o'clock the next day, an envelope containing $25.00 and we would then arrange its return to the victim.

This left the team to decide how to divide the payment among the dozen or so boys on the team. We heard stories of lunch money divided, monitor badges "pawned," borrowing from friends and a frantic scurrying around to collect the required sum lest their team be disbanded and all of their proposed matches forfeited. I repeat: principals had authority, and since students knew this, it was not often necessary to use it.

Yes, the money was there, and a shame-faced team presented it to the vendor. I think all of us breathed a sigh of relief and our boys learned a lesson.

Fight

Fighting with fists is bad enough, let alone fighting with guns. And yes, we certainly did have the problem of fighting in the schools. But it actually was another activity that finally brought satisfaction because it gave evidence of remarkable success in the solution of a problem; and again, I learned something. When we became principals of elementary schools in May 1948, both my husband and I found that our schools had many fights among the children. After recess periods, teachers had to spend time solving the problems that resulted from these fights. We decided to take drastic and immediate action and to do this, we appealed to the school staff to help us secure the cooperation of the parents. We took different approaches but obtained similar results.

My husband sent notes to the parents of the Drake School pupils inviting them to attend a meeting with the faculty on a specified Sunday afternoon at a local church for which he had been granted free use of the auditorium by the supportive pastor. The meeting was well attended and resulted in a cooperative plan for solving the problem. The children were informed of the new procedures and requirements by their parents at home, and the next day by their teachers.

At Willard, we mailed letters to each parent. Because of the large number, the letters were addressed by the upper grade students as a class activity. This saved the school staff a great deal of time, taught or reviewed a necessary skill, and to some degree involved the students. The approach was similar in the two schools. We emphasized that we were as concerned as the parents for the safety of our children. We could not protect any child, however, if any other child was permitted to attack him. Therefore, no one could be allowed to fight any other child for any reason. If there was a problem, the child should tell his parent or his teacher and we, together, would help him. Severe punishment would be given for any break in our "No Fighting" policy.

In addition, we had learned that fights were encouraged by "on-lookers" who sometimes urged the participants to continue by cheering, comments, etc. Our policy, therefore, declared spectators to be "participants" who would be punished along with the actual fighters. All of the children were now well informed of the letter content and our new motto, "We don't fight at Willard." It sounds a little corny but I would occasionally ask a child, "What is our new motto?" and always secure a proud answer. It sounds incredible but the fighting almost completely ceased at both schools.

Rules are Rules?

The incident which emphasized the importance of rules was one fight between two girls, one of whom had graduated from Willard in June and was attending the local high school. The other girl was an eighth-grade student in our school. We had started the "no-fighting policy" only in May and June right after our appointments to the schools and while both girls were still in attendance.

It seems that on a Friday or Saturday night, early in September, the eighth-grade girl had been allowed to go to a party with a boy whom both girls knew. The high school girl was very angry about this and, after school was dismissed on Monday afternoon, she came to our school to "beat up" the other girl. Since she was no longer a student at Willard, she was not concerned with our policy about fighting.

Someone ran into my office to say that there was a big fight on the street. I ran outside, hailed a passing car and secured a ride to the scene of the fighting, just around the corner on a side street. When we turned into the street, it was filled with students surrounding the two girls.

As the car approached and I stepped out, several children shouted, "There's Mrs. Lewis." The high school girl ran away and the spectators fled in all directions. They were well aware of the rule about spectators! Left standing alone, weeping, was our eighth grade girl; but then she, too, ran quickly away and the street was clear. No one wanted to be caught fighting or "supporting a fight" by being a spectator.

Now the question in many minds concerned our student who was involved–what would happen to her? This was the only fight which had occurred under our new regulations. Here is where I learned or decided something about "rules" that while necessary and important in society, rules should be applied and administered with some discretion, some fairness, and some "common sense" instead of in an iron-clad, insensitive manner.

I, with the faculty, announced that there had been a fight but our student was "not guilty." She was going home from school when she was attacked by another girl who had come to our school expressly for that purpose. Our student had tried to defend and protect herself, as anyone would be expected to do when attacked. Our rules could not be applied to her; so there was no reason for her to be punished. The older girl, however, was made an example for all to see, that fighting was still not allowed. Her high school principal agreed that she should return to our school so we could teach her again what she did not seem to have learned. Would we be able to do that now?

After a full week, I had a talk with the girl who "convinced" me that she had learned a big lesson and would never be the aggressor in such a situation again. In her presence, I called the high school principal to report our "progress" and suggested that we give her a chance to demonstrate this by returning her to her high school class. Thus, the case was closed and all was truly peaceful, even in the high school to which the girl returned. All the children "got the message."

Nowadays, such a "creative" and unofficial solution would not be tolerated, probably not even attempted. But, did it work? Without doubt! During the remainder of my two-year tenure, we had no problems whatsoever with children fighting.

Learning To Adjust

We

On one occasion, I was not the one who helped a new principal, but it happened in District Twenty while I was the superintendent. The appreciative principal told me the story. He was speaking to the staff at his first faculty meeting. He told them what he hoped to accomplish and some of the things that he hoped they would do to reach the goals he would set for the school. All went smoothly at the meeting, but afterward one of the male teachers stayed and requested a talk with him.

The teacher expressed pleasure at having him as their principal, full agreement on the goals to be set, and a pledge of cooperation. "I would like to see you succeed, but you made today what could be a fatal mistake. All afternoon you talked about your goals, your hopes, what you would do and what the rest of us could do. You used the words "I" and "you" but never the word "we." You set up a division between yourself and the rest of us. Unless we work together, we will accomplish very little and this division between us is a negative and destructive factor. I hope you understand and can make us feel a togetherness." It was my good fortune as the district superintendent, to have a frank, alert teacher who cared enough and was brave enough to speak, and a principal who was open to helpful advice and ready to benefit from it.

New *"Boss"*

The Chicago schools, for twelve or fifteen years before Dr. Hunt came in 1947, were governed by the political organizations, so strange things sometimes happened. One evening, the principal of a particular school received a telephone call at her home. A school administrator informed her that the Board of Education, in their meeting just concluded, had authorized her transfer to the principalship of another school (ours) and she was instructed to report there the next morning.

We learned later that no fault was to be found with her tenure, but that a sister of a prominent judge had become qualified to head a school for physically handicapped children and desired that position. The principal being removed was shocked and really devastated; she loved her school and had been getting along famously with parents, teachers, and children.

At our school, the capable principal had been promoted to a central office position; so we received the next morning, a weeping, demoralized "new" principal. We felt the injustice and had great sympathy for the principal, trying to make her welcome and to console her. Days went by and when she still did not seem to adjust, we began to think things like, "Come on now, we are not so bad," and "Well, it could be worse, you know," and we began to object to the fact that she was unwilling or unable to see the good qualities we thought we had. Perhaps our impatience began to show and she did begin to try to be "our" principal.

The New Principal

I had just been assigned to the principalship of Phillips High School, with over 3,000 students, and Phillips Elementary School (K-eighth grade) with nearly 1,100 youngsters. Needless to say, the two schools required a large faculty. The high school had been administered by a very talented lady who had been in charge of the school for 10 or 12 years and with whom the faculty had become "comfortable" until her retirement; so I was just "accepted." For months, I was "the new principal." On one occasion, after many months in the school when someone gave me a key to the store room in the main office, I told friends I believed that I was really going to be principal after all, really accepted.

Handling Hostility

I was the adjustment teacher for a few years during my career. At the time, the Physical Education teacher and I were the only teachers on staff without a full class all of the time and the only ones beside the principal with Masters degrees, which perhaps made her a bit insecure. It seemed that the principal began to single us out for unusual treatment. She would send a child to summon one of us to the office for the most trivial question or information, sometimes several times in a day.

I was complaining about the principal one day in the presence of the minister of our church. He looked at me disapprovingly and said, "I am surprised at you. Do you mean to tell us that you cannot win that woman?"

I was shocked; he seemed to feel that I was responsible for allowing the condition to persist. He was our pastor, and we respected his leadership and guidance. It gave me food for thought and I realized that, except for the first welcoming days, I had not been trying to "win that woman;" I was too busy resenting what we thought was her hostile attitude.

I deliberately started going into her office with a pleasant smile and apparent willingness to hear her comments or answer her questions. I was surprised at how quickly her attitude seemed to change. I recalled my mother's admonition: "A soft answer turneth away wrath." That may not always be true, but it certainly worked in this case.

As the months went by, it was this principal who was one of those persons urging me to take the coming examination for certification as a school principal. She and my district superintendent brought books they thought I should read, and she began to take me as her guest to the principals' luncheons in our district. As a result, when I did become a principal, I was not a stranger in meetings with other principals. I was always grateful to that lady and to the pastor of our church who alerted me to a better way of dealing with problems in human relationships.

I Don't Expect
To Begin Now

Some teachers resisted the principal's efforts as a "teacher of teachers." In one case, I visited the classroom of a math teacher newly assigned to our high school. I entered quietly, smiled, softly said "Good morning," proceeded to the rear of the classroom and took a seat. I expected the teacher to continue with the class procedure, but instead, he stopped and turned to me with a question, "Did you want something?" I replied negatively and said that I had only come to observe for a short period. His reply was, "Well, I have never had anyone observe my teaching and I don't expect to begin now!" Amazed, but aware of the startled students' full attention, I smiled and said, "Well, that's unfortunate, but (firmly) I guess you will have to begin now. You may go on with the lesson." Of course, he complied and after what I thought gave me a good picture of what was being taught and learned, I quietly left the room.

This same teacher had asked if he might teach a class in adagio dancing as an after school recreational activity. The group was soon organized, but finding a place was a problem and the only one available was the stage of the auditorium. I stopped in one day to visit the class and they were doing the acrobatics very well that seemed to go with that kind of dance.

However, to my horror, the newly painted back wall of the stage was covered with footprints where the "gym shoes" of the students had landed as they leaped or ran and pivoted a return. To me, the wall looked terrible and my reaction was magnified by the fact that it had taken several years for me to get the authorities to provide in the budget for painting the worn, faded, and soiled stage background.

I was not happy with his instructional skills when I visited his classroom several other times and I decided that we would be better off without this teacher, especially when he said, "I am surprised that you are upset. I would think you, as principal of this big school, would have more and better things to do, or worry about, than footprints on the back wall."

Well aware that he was going to be marked "Unsatisfactory," the teacher applied for a transfer and was accepted at a neighboring school. That principal said that perhaps the "very unorthodox" teacher would fit in with some he already had. I was relieved to be rid of this man whom I felt I had not really reached at all.

High I.Q.

I remember serving as the "adjustment" teacher at Washington Elementary school when we had an interesting new little girl come to enroll. She was 7 1/2 years but had never been to school. When reported by neighbors and investigated by the truant officer, we learned that the mother, a high school graduate, had been teaching her informally at home and had seen no need to send her to school since she was "already reading" and playing the piano. As adjustment teacher it was my responsibility to test the little girl and recommend placement. I gave her a first grade reader, then a third and finally a book which our eighth grade classes used. She read each of these with ease and was able to explain clearly what she had read.

In formal testing we found her to be at eighth or ninth grade in reading, seventh grade in spelling and fifth grade in mathematics. When the school psychologist came and gave her a "Standford-Binet," the official test for intelligence, her score was something like 212. "Normal" is around 100.

During the test, I was seated quietly in a far corner of the large classroom (which I used for my office, for testing, some remedial work and coaching of foreign students in English). I heard the psychologist ask the child if she could give her the names of any books she had read. The girl asked, "How do you want them? In the order in which I read them?" The tester replied that any order would be satisfactory. I decided to make a note of the child's response so I quickly got a sheet of what we called "foolscap" and was ready. The child asked, "Do you want the authors?" The tester replied that she would be glad to hear them if the child would like to name them. To my amazement, that child reeled off the names of books and authors in groups of seven until I had filled the front and half of the back of my sheet of paper (approximately 10 inch, lined). She explained that adults could borrow five books at a time and children could borrow two from the public library. Her mother would get five books and, with her own two, she would have seven books from each weekly trip to the library.

With all of her brilliance, however, the child had no "social skills." She had never played with other children and was fearful climbing the stairs in the school. For this, she blamed her mother because the mother was so protective, always holding her hand and saying "Be careful." The other children were at first inclined to laugh at her but soon recognized how "smart" she really was and accepted her. She, herself, sized up the situation and made a rapid adjustment and began making friends.

But what to do with such a child? The principal told her and her mother that since she was able to do math at a fifth grade level, we would send her to a fifth grade when they were doing arithmetic and for reading, we would program her sometimes to read to the kindergarten and first grade classes. For her home room, however, we explained that she needed to be with children of her own age and she would have art, music, physical education, health and other subjects and activities with the third grade.

This girl was a lovely child, not conceited or overbearing, aware of her ability but also of her weaknesses. She was very inept on the playground or with physical exercises and she refrained from sports activities. After graduation from our school and the neighboring high school we heard that she had been accepted at one of the most prestigious colleges for women. This was certainly the brightest pupil with whom I ever worked.

One unsatisfactory element of a teaching career is that after you have helped a student to learn and perhaps to acquire or strengthen his or her understanding of right and wrong, how to get along with and treat others, to develop worthwhile goals, etc., you often lose track of them and never know how their lives "turned out" and what they were able to accomplish. Only for a few of your many students do you derive that satisfaction.

My Father Wears His Hat

Because it was well known that the principal had the authority for any necessary discipline, the students rarely challenged me directly. On one occasion, however, one young man did so. I was walking with another individual in a corridor of the building when I noticed a lad approaching us wearing his hat, something which was "taboo" in our school.

I was engaged in an interesting and important conversation so I merely put out my hand as the boy neared and turned toward him expecting to see the hat removed and a shame-faced expression on the boy's face. I expected to simply nod and motion for him to keep going. Instead, to my surprise, he was standing with his hat on and a look of defiance on his face. I said, "Oh, son, didn't you understand? I meant for you to take your hat off."

He replied, "My father wears his hat in the house."

I realized that he had cleverly placed me in a situation where I could either forget about our school rule or I could be charged with criticism of his father. I asked the boy to wait for me in my office where, a few minutes later, I had to extricate myself from a difficult spot. I said, "You say your father wears his hat in the house? Well, let's not be too critical of him. We don't know what happened when he was growing up and probably his teachers did not teach him properly and that's too bad. You are more fortunate, however, and your teachers have taught you and will continue to teach you whatever will help you later, so you will have to take your hat off." I paused while he removed his cap, then asked, "You understand?"

"Yes, Mrs. Lewis," he replied, and I simply asked where he was going and if he needed a "pass" to get there, and the incident was closed.

Respect

75

Faculty Meeting

I remember when I held my first high school faculty meeting. We met in the auditorium because of the size of the group and as it was, I had learned, the custom. All of the teachers were seated near the front of the room and the male shop teachers were seated together as a group.

When I arose and greeted the faculty, I began to address them briefly, as planned, and to introduce myself and my hopes for my tenure there. I had hardly begun, however, when I heard subdued voices from the section where the shop teachers were seated and, to my surprise, found that some of those in the front row were turned around in their seats to face their colleagues in the second row. "So much for their interest in me or whatever I had to say" was what their attitude implied.

I kept on speaking briefly and then in the middle of a sentence, I stopped, turned my gaze toward the inattentive teachers and waited, staring at the group. It only took seconds before they became aware of the situation, turned around and gave respectful attention for the remainder of the session, while I picked up my half-finished sentence, completed it and the rest of my presentation. I learned, "You do not ignore or tolerate such disrespect" and my teachers learned that you do not give such disrespect; it will not be tolerated by this principal.

Why did these incidents end well? I believe it was because they, children and teachers, knew I had the authority to take some stronger action if I was forced to do so. Because of that, they were rarely tempted to require any severe action from me. Partly for that reason, being principal at Phillips was a joy and a really pleasurable experience.

Respect Required

I recall one incident when I was principal of Willard Elementary School, during my first two years as a school administrator. The school clerk complained to me that she was having great difficulty with the figures from a particular teacher's "Summary Sheet," a monthly report of student membership and attendance. I asked the teacher to come and see if I could be of help. The teacher stormed into my office, highly indignant, and in angry tones informed me that she had been taught by a particular professor at the Teachers' College and she had always done her report in the same manner. Now, I had known this teacher for some time in the social college groups; but I addressed her formally, saying "Mrs.—, have a seat and listen carefully. Do not ever, I repeat, ever, come into this office using that tone or manner of voice as long as I am principal of this school. If Professor— taught you, he either was in error or you did not learn correctly. The method you are using is wrong and your results are wrong. You will have to learn and use the method all of the other teachers use. Is that clear?"

Her response was immediate. She changed from her hostile attitude and, smiling, said to me, "Oh, now Virginia, you know me. You know I don't mean any harm. I just blow off a lot of steam. Now you just tell me what to do and that will be the end of it." I wanted to laugh but instead, I took my pencil and clearly outlined her future procedure and when we finished and I was sure that she understood, we completed (corrected) her "Summary Sheet" for the clerk and all was well thereafter. This reinforced what I had already learned: that there were times when an administrator must assert the prerogatives of that office and require respect and cooperation, yourself giving respect all of the while.

Do You Know What He Did To Me?

I recall a funny incident happening one day. A tiny little teacher rushed into my office, very much agitated. Behind her loomed the huge figure of one of the shop teachers. He was also in charge of distributing audio-visual equipment to different classes as requested by individual teachers. He had a crew of boys, organized into a "club," who performed this service under his direction.

On this day, when the teacher met her class prepared to use some visual equipment and material as a vital part of her instruction, the boys had failed to deliver the necessary instrument. Usually, the boys and their sponsor did a superb job, but this day was different. The disappointed, and perhaps angry, teacher had rushed to the shop teacher's classroom to complain and request immediate service. Probably because of her manner, the male teacher made no response; he only listened.

Furious, in my office, she asked, "Do you know what he did to me? Right in front of my face, while I was talking to him, he deliberately reached into his shirt pocket and turned his hearing aid off." Completely frustrated, she had rushed to my office to report him and perhaps have him chastised. It was not a bit funny to her, but it was a comical scene: this tiny lady, waving her hands and "breathing fire" and behind her, this giant of a man looking calm and somewhat amused, but also somewhat sheepish. It didn't take too long for a peaceful conclusion: Soothing and understanding words from me and apologies from the shop teacher brought a return to normal. The equipment was rescheduled.

My Name Is Mrs. Lewis

I always made an effort to get to know each of my students and my colleagues by name. So I don't know why I was reluctant to confront the Superintendent about such a simple issue. He had been with us quite a while and continued to address me as "Mrs. Phillips," using the name of the high school where I was the principal. Finally, I grew tired of this and one day when we were alone for a few minutes, I responded to his erroneous greeting by saying with a big smile, "I'm going to get someone to introduce me to you. You see my name is really Mrs. Lewis." He sputtered a little and said, "Oh, of course," as others joined us. From that time on, however, I was "Mrs. Lewis" and I think I earned his respect. It was he who later selected me, or at least, approved my appointment as Assistant Superintendent.

Don't Be Silly

I learned a terrific lesson when I first went to Phillips High School as principal. Some of the teachers had been my college classmates, others were members of my sorority, my church, or my bridge club. One such teacher was the chairman of the Physical Education department and teacher of the splendid Modern Dance group. I was chatting with her informally one day, and after she had made some remark, I laughingly said, "Oh, don't be silly." I believe her comment had been a modest denial of her exceptional talent and I think my response was to imply that, of course, the beautiful dancing of the students was due to her skill.

However, to my surprise, her smile disappeared and she said in a very somber, formal tone, "Well, I hope I am not silly. I try never to be silly. I hope you don't think I am." She was very serious and I was truly at a loss for words. I hastened, to the best of my ability, to assure her that I had simply used a common expression to say that her leadership of the group should not be depreciated. I apologized and apparently convinced her that I had not realized that such an expression could be offensive and was in no way applicable to my estimate of her. Fortunately, this incident played no part in our future relationship. Perhaps she forgot it, but I never did, and it influenced my future behavior.

I was made to realize, and to my benefit, that we have to be careful of the words we use. They have the power to hurt and to misinform; once uttered, they cannot be recalled.

I also had to rethink the relationship of the principal and her teachers. I was apparently forgetting that I was not her club member, or fellow classmate. I was in her mind and, of course, actually, her "superior," "boss," "evaluator." Friends we could and should still be, but in our work relationships, I had to realize that there was a different setting and one that required a more careful stance on my part.

As the drama teacher put it to her actors, "While you are on stage, you never get out of character. You do not have friends in the audience; you remain in your role until the end of the play." I had the P.E. teacher and the Drama teacher to thank for another good lesson.

Expectations

Wouldn't You Rather Drop The Course?

I liked being a student at Northwestern University. It was summer and the first day for my introduction to Trigonometry. I was feeling good about myself. Math was one of my majors, and I was working on my degree. I knew I had chosen the right path ever since first grade. Times tables had been a snap for me. Long division gave me no headaches. Algebra and geometry were puzzles that I loved figuring out. My teachers tended to make me a teacher's pet (which I didn't like), but I knew they thought I was good. And I was.

I took my seat at the front of the class. As soon as the professor had taken roll, he beckoned to me to come up to his desk. It was only a few steps, but several thoughts went through my head as I stepped up there. What was wrong? As a black woman, my antennae was attuned to special vibrations. Had my files been misplaced? Had I not filled out some necessary paperwork? Or was it something uglier than that?

"Miss Lewis," he began, and I studied his eyes behind their steel-rimmed glasses, trying to answer my own questions. "Miss Lewis," he began again.
"Yessir."

"In my years of teaching I have never had a person of your color–and gender–who has succeeded in my course, and I thought . . ." (did I detect a sigh?) "that perhaps you would rather drop the course than have a failing grade on your record."

Failure! Never happen! I was incensed. Who did he think he was deciding before he knew anything about me that I was going to fail? I could feel my palms getting sweaty, and I dug my nails into them to help me "keep my cool." My response came out in the polite manner my mother had always insisted upon. "Don't be disrespectful, Virginia. You can't afford to let your anger get the best of you." Her words repeated over and over in my head were a saving grace.

"Professor Simmons," I said, making sure my tone was as level as possible. I was shaking. "Math is my second major, and "Trig" is essential for my graduation. I have no choice." He nodded and indicated that I should return to my seat. I don't remember much else about that first class.

To give the devil his due, Professor Simmons was a good instructor, and he treated me no differently than he did the rest of the class. At the end of the semester, he again called me up to his desk after I had proven my worth and earned a solid A.

"Miss Lewis," he said, and this time I was not troubled. I knew he would have something good to say to me. "Miss Lewis, it was a pleasure to have you in my class, " he said. "If you ever need a recommendation, don't hesitate to call on me."

Supervision And Administration At N.U.

Another recollection, also at Northwestern University, in the evening school, was in a class called "Supervision and Administration." I was teaching in the public schools of Chicago and also seeking a degree in Education and the professor of the class was a man who was an Assistant Superintendent in the Chicago Public School System.

He called me to his desk at the first class session and asked why I was taking this course. He said, "You know, you can never be an administrator in the Chicago Public Schools." He did not explain why, nor did I need to ask, as I knew he referred to the past history of racial bias in the school system. My husband learned later, for example, that the president of the Board of Education was said to have declared, "No black man will ever be a principal of a school and supervise white women while I am in office." Black women fared little better. I replied to the professor that I was too near my degree to change majors and that I would like to continue even though I understood his question.

To the credit of both of these men, I must add a footnote. They both said they enjoyed having me in their class. The first offered to write a recommendation if I ever needed one. After the administration class, I saw and heard no more from the second professor until, many years later, when I was promoted to District Superintendent, I received a letter of congratulation!

"I Seen The Paper"

Another case both amused and saddened me when I was Assistant Superintendent. A young substitute teacher visited me in the central office to complain about his new teaching assignment. At the close of the school year, he had been working at a school which he liked and to which he expected to return for the fall term. Instead, he was sent elsewhere and he was very much disappointed. I listened with sympathy until he said, "I know the principal asked for me. I seen the paper."

His grammar shocked and displeased me (once an English major), as he talked on, revealing many errors. Our subsequent discussion saddened me even more. He thought, since he was a teacher of mathematics that his use of correct or incorrect grammar was of little importance. I attempted to persuade him to the contrary. I told him that I was in a dilemma about recommending his return to the first school, a community of well-educated, concerned parents, who would be very unhappy with the teacher's faulty grammar. However, I could not recommend him for work at the second school, which was in a neighborhood of poor, somewhat illiterate parents, whose children had little opportunity except at school, to learn correct grammar. Only from their teachers could they learn skills to prepare them for a better life than their parents had.

Unfortunately, and this is one of the disappoint-
ments of teaching, I did not learn what happened in this
case. I could only hope that our conference was meaning-
ful to him and that he accepted my advice to enroll in an
English class or secure a tutor who would help him correct
his deficiencies.

Where Is Your Teacher?

There was an incident, which made me dissatisfied with myself as well as with a teacher newly assigned to our school. Because we were overcrowded and operating on what was considered an extended day, our school started very early and ran late in the afternoon. R.O.T.C was during what we called "zero period," beginning at 7:30 a.m., and tenth period ended after 4:00 p.m. Then there were basketball games and other activities which ended even later. We agreed that the Assistant Principal would be "in charge" early and I would arrive about 9:00 a.m. and stay until all activities ended.

One morning, when I arrived and entered from the parking area, I walked through our long, first-floor corridor toward the office, which was in the front of the building. Glancing now and then into a classroom as I passed, something caught my attention. In one room the students seemed to be talking in small groups, reading, or dozing. I entered the room to see what was going on. I asked, "Where is your teacher?" and was told that he had not arrived. I was truly shocked when one student added, "This is the third morning he hasn't shown up." I was horrified and felt fully responsible. How could this have happened without my knowledge? Where had our system failed? I felt the weight of inadequacy when one of my classes had no teacher for three days! I took it as a personal shortcoming.

Fortunately, I had a District Superintendent with whom I felt comfortable. When I reached the office, my first action was to call him. My first question to him was, "Do you know where you can get a new principal for this school – one who knows what's going on?" I then told him of my discovery and he understood why I was so upset.

His response calmed me and restored a little faith in myself. He said, "Well, let's have a conference with this teacher. He was transferred to your school as a "second chance" after being marked "unsatisfactory" elsewhere. But there is a bright side to this. If this had happened at some schools, everyone would have known that a class was without a teacher. Those pupils would have been roaming the halls and generally making noise and creating problems. The students should be congratulated and you can feel proud, as I do, that the school is so well disciplined."

Incidentally, when I had a conference later that day with the teacher, I asked to see his lesson plans for that day. He submitted a book of plans, but the dates were for use several years earlier. If he used it at all, he was using plans written years before for another class. Needless to say, we were relieved of his presence on our faculty through some action by the District Superintendent after conferences and approvals from the proper authorities.

Signing The Payroll

An incident somewhat related arose during a meeting of the general superintendent and his staff. The principal had refused to sign the payroll for a teacher who claimed illness when the principal knew he had taken the day off for some personal activities. The teacher was protesting this action. The superintendent was new and very formidable. He seemed annoyed that the principal had made an issue of this case by not signing. Perhaps because I, as principal, had been faced with such an issue, I spoke up on behalf of this principal. By doing so, I think I amazed my fellow administrators and probably the superintendent also. In retrospect, I was amazed myself that I had dared to take issue with him. I merely commented that I could understand the principal because when she affixed her signature it was equivalent to a declaration by her that all items contained therein were correct and true. The superintendent simply nodded and said, "Yes, that's true," and dropped the matter.

Shopping

When I was the principal at Phillips High School, we were planning special decorations for some big event. The committee of teachers had worked hard to finish in time, but at the last minute they found they had run short of some badly needed item. I volunteered to hop in my car and go purchase the item since all of them were due in their classrooms.

At the store, I found the right counter and looked up into the face of the customer on the other side. It was one of the teachers from our school, one who had called in that morning to say that she couldn't come to work because she was too ill. What a surprise for me and what a shock for her! I greeted her but hastened to take the items I needed to the cashier and depart.

Her embarrassment seemed to be "punishment enough." I never mentioned the incident to her and, of course, she did not claim illness as her reason for absence. Sometimes, I had learned, a principal, teacher, or parent has to sense when the "mission has been accomplished," and therefore, when to speak and when to be silent.

I'm Going To Be Ill

One Friday, I was standing in the office when teachers were signing out at 3:15 p.m., and I heard one teacher say to the clerk, "I won't be here Monday. I'm going to be ill." We were allowed to have a number of days during the year when, if you were ill, no pay would be deducted from your salary. I made it clear to the clerk that I would not approve the payroll for a teacher who had proclaimed illness several days in advance. This information was passed on and I was not asked to sign something which I knew to be wrong.

Bending The Rules

I must confess, however, that with reference to a couple of school system rules, I was not very meticulous. There was one rule which said that a child must attend school in the district in which the parent lived. In general, that is a logical requirement. I had two very superior teachers for whom this rule, if applied, would cause a hardship. Their situations were similar; living far from school, they would need to employ someone to care for their children before and after school. The only alternative to avoid this expense would be to transfer, if they could, to schools near their homes.

Such a transfer might not be available, and if it was, our school would be deprived of two superior teachers. I decided that if the attendance of these three children caused a problem, or if someone brought the fact of their attendance to my attention officially, I would have to take some action. Until such time, however, I decided to be totally ignorant of their presence. Nothing transpired to force us to lose these teachers or to create difficulties for them. I do believe that rules or laws are necessary to our society and that they should be obeyed; however, I think, there are occasional exceptions and that our laws and rules have to be administered with good judgment. I felt justified because it was a solution that provided the best conditions for our school pupils, the two teachers and their three children.

I was motivated by the same considerations when I failed to be aware that two of our splendid teachers had married and that there was a rule that husband and wife could not teach at the same school. I am not proud that I acted (or failed to act) without regard to these regulations. My real concern for my faculty and pupils overrode everything else. These personal experiences probably made me more understanding when dealing with other teachers or students who really had a beneficial reason for a failure to comply with a school rule.

You Took Not One Note

In another case, fortunately not in my district, the new high school principal had a less pleasant experience. It was his first meeting with a group of parents, and different ones had spoken to tell him some of the problems about which they were greatly concerned.

The principal had listened and thanked each one politely. One parent rose, however, as the meeting drew toward the end and said words to this effect: "I am greatly disappointed and feel that this meeting has been a waste of our time. I feel that you don't plan to do any of the things we proposed or try to solve any of the problems. It is true that you listened; but it isn't possible for you to remember everything and you never took one note; you have not kept anything as a reminder. I, for one, am very much displeased."

I think the Bible says we should "avoid the appearance of evil." This new principal did not realize how he was giving the impression, however false, of not intending to bother with the complaints and recommendations of the parents. Another lesson learned.

You Are On A Scholarship

I recall incidents, particularly with freshmen, or new students, when I would remind them that all of them were there on scholarships and therefore had a responsibility to do their best. "Scholarships?" The surprised students thought I had surely made a mistake.

I would explain by asking questions without waiting for an answer. "Who bought your books? Did your parents pay tuition as they would in a private school? Where does the money come from to maintain this building and to pay the staff and teachers? The taxpayers of Chicago pay for your education. If you fail a grade, it costs them twice for you to have another chance. You have a great opportunity to attend a free public school and a great responsibility to succeed." Suddenly, some of the students, at least, grasped a new concept about school, their education and themselves (their role). Sometimes I would tell students, "This is an educational institution, not a park or a playground. This is where you come to learn and it is our responsibility to help you learn and see that you do. It is your responsibility to get your education and do your best."

The School Is Closed

The single most influential event in relation to my teaching career happened when I was just 15 years old. I was to graduate in June from Shortridge High School in Indianapolis, Indiana, the city of my birth. Screaming headlines in the newspapers one day bore surprising and alarming news. The Legislature had discovered that there was no legislative permission for the establishment of the Teachers' Normal School, which had been operating for years. Their solution was to close the school, allowing those presently in attendance to complete their two-year course but, of course, enrolling no new students.

We were speechless; what would I do? My father was a clergyman, pastoring in a low-income community and paid accordingly, and my mother was only partly employed by conducting a beauty parlor in our home. Tuition at nearby Butler University for four years seemed an impossibility. Though my grades were excellent, we never heard anything about scholarships and anyway, my parents thought that I was too young to go away to a Normal School in another part of the state.

Chicago: A Turn in the Road

Fortunately, my father's niece came to our rescue. She had a home and family in Chicago with two children older than I and one younger. She suggested that I come to Chicago and attend the free Normal School there. I could share a room with her older daughter who was a student at the Chicago Normal School; I could share household chores with the other children as a member of the family; my cousin and her husband would serve as foster parents, and my father could pay her a very, very small fee for my food, my personal and school needs.

What an opportunity and what a turning point in my life! I had always planned to be a teacher; even as a small child "playing school" with my neighbors, I was always the teacher. Leaving home, however, had never entered my mind or the minds of my parents. Fortunately, I knew these cousins well because they spent every summer with their grandmother, my aunt, and we played together very often.

There was no other choice and we were grateful for this one, so September found me enrolling in the Junior College while "establishing residence" and preparing to take the entrance examination for the Normal School in late December.

I was blessed again by passing that examination and in February, I was enrolled and started on the preparation phase of my long teaching career in Chicago.

Test Time

Decades ago, the district superintendent visited the school periodically to ascertain that the children were learning as they should. We didn't yet have many standardized tests. On one visit, he gave a test. He had me distribute spelling paper (a narrow, ruled sheet), and he called out the words from a list he had brought with him. He had selected the words from the spelling book for that grade. He took the papers with him and I guess they helped him to decide on the quality of instruction I was providing.

Sing!

On another occasion, he visited my classroom when I was teaching seventh grade. This time, he was checking their progress in music. He had with him several sheets torn from a music book. With my class attentive, he selected several students (at random) to whom he distributed his song sheets. The selected pupils were after a few minutes of study, expected to stand and give the key in which the song was written, and then sing it using the syllables "do, re, me, etc." Then the child was to sing the song using "loo" or "la" and, finally sing the words. Talk about a scary experience! I am not a music major, nor a skilled pianist, but my children did very well. That training at the Teacher's College in "how-to-teach" music paid off well. One corner of the blackboard was often devoted to a "Song Study," frequently changed as it was mastered by the class.

Trouble At School

Heart Attack

One incident did not end very fortunately. A teacher rushed to my office to alert us that a young lad had collapsed on the third floor and the teacher believed the boy was dead. He had a history of heart problems. He had been out to lunch and upon his return had hurried up two flights of stairs to his locker. He had just removed his books when he fell. Though we had several lunch periods, our cafeteria could not accommodate all of our students and some chose to go out in the neighborhood to the equivalent of McDonald's, Burger King, etc. This incident could be considered my most frightening experience at that school.

Alcohol

Some incidents had surprise endings. We were privileged to have a Social Center on Friday nights. This was an effort to provide some wholesome activity for the students' pleasure. The Board of Education provided supervision, a dance band and refreshments. The Assistant Principal was already in charge of this program when I became Principal, so I rarely attended.

On one Friday afternoon as I was walking in the corridor, students were moving from class to class during the time period allocated for that purpose. As one young man attempted to get a book from his locker, a bottle of whiskey fell to the floor and broke, almost at my feet. Of course the student was distressed and proclaimed at once, "That wasn't mine, that wasn't mine!"

As calmly as possible I told him to come with me. In my office, he began to explain that another young man who was not a student at the school was the owner of the alcohol. He said the young man was planning to attend the Social Center that evening but thought he might not be able to enter with the bottle. He had asked the student, a friend, to keep it in his locker until dance time. He said the young man "hung around" an eating place across the street and had just given it to him at lunch time.

I asked if the young man was still there and, looking from my window, the student said that he was one of a group loitering there. I suggested that he "cut" his next class, with my permission, and go outside and join his friends. I promised him that I would never reveal that he had been the one to identify the young man with whom he would talk about the broken bottle, thereby allowing me to see which young man it was. The student felt, I thought, that he could fully trust me to keep my promise and he eagerly agreed and left the office.

To my surprise, when I checked, there were no young men loitering as had frequently been the case. And to my greater surprise, the student did not return. We can only guess that perhaps there was no "outside friend" and that he did not want to confess that he had purchased the bottle of alcohol to share at the Social Center. Our efforts to locate him proved fruitless.

A Screwdriver

Another incident involving alcohol occurred when two very nice boys, both very good students, arrived at school one morning quite intoxicated. It seems that they had heard that there was a very good drink called a screwdriver made of orange juice and vodka. They were very curious and decided to try it. On this particular morning, they met early and purchased orange juice at the grocery store. They then persuaded a man loitering somewhere nearby to purchase the alcohol for them. Gleefully they found a secluded spot to enjoy their secret drink. They had no idea what the effects of the drink would be and that they would be obvious.

Of course, they were brought to the principal's office and their parents were called. When the parents arrived, we sat down together to decide what to do. We agreed that the boys could not, for their sake and the sake of other students, go without some punishment; but we agreed, also, that whatever we did should provide a positive lesson to the boys, severe enough so that they would long remember it, but not a permanent condemnation.

We agreed on a school suspension and a "grounding" at home. They would be responsible for school assignments, but would miss class instruction and all school and social activities. Restricted for the suspension period to the house, the parents vetoed visits or phone calls from friends, television and games. Home chores were added such as cleaning the attic, garage and basement, scrubbing baths and kitchens, even painting an area. Being good students, there was no permanent damage to their classwork and to their self-esteem. We had no other incidents of intoxication.

What Do You Have?

I recall a big surprise, one which happened on the next day after a social worker had enrolled a boy who was being transferred from a "juvenile facility." She believed that his behavior would now be acceptable in a regular school. The boy was brought to my office for fighting. I sat down and talked with him. He exhibited great anger as he spoke of another boy whom he had encountered only the day before. He finally said, "Oh, I'll get him. I'm ready for him."

I think he must have patted his chest or made some gesture that alerted me, so I asked quickly, "What do you mean? What do you have?"

Whereupon, he reached down into his buttoned jacket and withdrew a long butcher knife. To say that I was shocked would be an understatement. Without thinking, and very unwisely, I reached for the knife and, fortunately, he didn't resist. I think the forcefulness of my reaction startled him. Though I didn't expect a weapon, I guess my quick response wasn't what he expected and it unnerved him.

I called the case worker and told her that I feared that the boy still had some serious problems that needed lots of help (professional) which our facilities could not provide. The unfortunate lad was removed from our school at once by the case worker who had enrolled him. We were very sorry, but felt that we couldn't help him. I had to accept the fact that we couldn't win them all.

Murder

One terrible experience occurred when I was a District Superintendent. I had remained at home that day because of a severe cold. About four o'clock in the afternoon, I answered my phone to a call from the police who informed me that there had been a tragic incident at one of the schools in my district. I rushed to the school and learned that a teacher had been attacked and killed.

She had remained after school (as many conscientious teachers sometimes did) to complete some work and she had gone into our book storage room. A fourteen-year-old boy had slipped back into the building and surprised and attacked her. It was a large building and no one heard a sound; but the clerk, checking the "sign-in" sheet, noted that this teacher had not "signed out" and asked one of the janitors to investigate.

I do not recall how they discovered the boy nor how the case terminated. I do not remember a great coverage by the press, but it caused our teachers to forego after-school work in the buildings unless they were protected by the presence of others. We learned of an unsuspected danger.

Reporters And Policemen

I learned something else about newspaper
reporters and policemen, and how individuals in these
jobs can be obstreperous or noble. The principal of the
school where the teacher was killed had a small office
(really a section of the main office partitioned off) because
of overcrowding. After the trauma of this experience, she
attempted to seclude herself for a few minutes. A persist-
ent reporter, however, with his camera, obtained from
somewhere a step-ladder which he placed outside of the
principal's office. He attempted to climb the ladder and
take a picture from above the partition. He was firmly dis-
suaded from doing so by me and my angered staff.

He, or another reporter with a camera shortly after
the discovery had attempted to take a picture of the
teacher lying on the floor with her skirts lifted and clothes
in disarray. To his great credit, a young policeman stopped
him. He called for a blanket and, himself, covered the
teacher's body. He said, "I may lose my job for this but if I
do, so be it. I cannot bear the thought of having this lady's
children and relatives open the morning paper and see
her in this condition as I saw her here." I could not get his
name but have always considered him a sensitive, caring
person–a "hero" on the job. The police then took control
of the situation and even we could not approach the scene.
We gave thanks for that noble young policeman.

What Is Your Choice?

I learned that most children respond positively when treated "kindly and firmly" but with respect. On occasions when I had a boy or girl referred to me for wholly unacceptable behavior or even for failing grades, the exchange went something like this: "Would you like to continue at this school? We would like to keep you, but there are certain rules about attendance, behavior and learning that everybody has to follow and our responsibility is to see that this is done. Now you have a choice to stay and follow the rules or be transferred elsewhere. The evening school, where you would be with adults who are serious about learning might be a good placement for you. What would you like to do?" Invariably, the choice was to remain at Phillips with the understanding between us that there would be conformity to the rules and standards of our school. This procedure was not needed many times because the students and their parents knew that I did have the authority to separate unruly students from the school. As a result, I was rarely challenged to use that authority; the children wanted to stay at Phillips.

FIRE!

I might not call my experiences hair-raising, but several incidents at the high school were not very pleasant. I was in my office one day when a student rushed in saying that the auditorium was on fire. Several of us rushed to the auditorium, which was directly across the corridor from my office. Of course, we called the fire department and rang the alarm for the students and teachers to vacate the building. Our carefully practiced fire drills "paid off"; the building was vacated quickly and in an orderly fashion. Soon the blaze was extinguished and classes returned to normal. Thankfully, the only damage was to the stage curtains.

The Ceiling Fell

On another occasion, a teacher rushed into the office to report an accident on the third floor. A piece of the ceiling in the gymnasium had fallen and struck a boy who seemed to be badly wounded. "His scalp has been split open and I think I can see brain tissue," said the teacher. I cannot remember how I climbed those long flights of stairs, but I was very quickly on the third floor and in the gym. We had someone call for help before leaving the office and help soon arrived. Fortunately, the young man, a good student and fine athlete, was not so seriously wounded as the teacher had thought. The wound was superficial and the young man was able to return to school in a couple of days and had no later related problems.

Lessons In Multi-Culture

Race, Religion, Nationality

I also learned a lot about interracial and intergroup relations and attitudes. After a year of working as a "substitute teacher," I was first assigned to a school where in the main building and the branch (a city block away) there were approximately 80 teachers of whom four, like me, were black (or "colored," "Negro," or "African-American," as we have been called at various periods). Many of the parents were immigrants and they were of 80% Italian, 10% Greek, and 10% Polish and other backgrounds, but as a teacher, I discovered an important fact. These were not white children, or Italian or Greek children. Those were MY children, and to them (and their parents) I was their teacher. I soon found that with many of the teachers, I was an individual, a colleague, with little or no regard for color or ethnic origin.

I could never again accept group classifications such as, "Italians do this," or "are like that," or "Greeks do this," or "are like that." I am always urged to challenge people who use those expressions to categorize groups. I had been taught at home (though in a segregated setting) to respect and evaluate each individual as a separate person. My experience as a teacher supported that teaching and made it an enriching reality in my life. Colleagues of other races, religions, and nationalities became life-long and best friends.

Stand For Principles

The following story illustrates how one principal was responsible for a great change in the lives of many children, parents and teachers. My friend, Laconia, was sent to this school as a substitute for a teacher on leave. Laconia was a very attractive young woman who was African American; the students and other teachers were white.

When the children went home for lunch (which was customary) several of them did not return. The next day, a large number did not come to school, and by the third day, a large number of students were missing. The principal had several options. He could release Mrs. Wilson and call the "Substitute Center" of the school system and ask for a different substitute or he could act according to his beliefs. He said, "We say we live in a democracy so it might as well start here." He sent a letter to every parent restating school rules regarding absences and then stated that the very competent new teacher would be teaching that class for the rest of the semester (about 3 months) and except for serious illness, each child would be expected to be in attendance on Monday.

Well, the parents had no alternative; the classroom was full on Monday and at the end of the term, the children were sadly saying "good-bye" with hugs and tears. Some parents stopped by to thank Mrs. Wilson and several sent her notes or farewell gifts.

As a teacher, I learned again what it means to stand firm for a principle. That principal changed many lives, parents and children and perhaps others whose lives they touched.

Feeling Free

We never thought in terms of patriotism; this was our country, and as difficult as it was for us at times, it was the only country we had known. But I can tell you of an experience we shall never forget. From a friend whom we met at the farm while vacationing in Michigan, we were motivated to make a trip to Mexico where he spent time every year and had many Mexican friends. We had to plan our trip very carefully because, in those days, it was difficult for persons of color to find hotel accommodations. Friends helped us; several wrote ahead to what would be good stopping places and where they had family members or close friends living. We were welcomed at these stops, made some new friends, and gratefully proceeded on our drive to Mexico.

Then an amazing and wonderful thing happened. We crossed the border! Suddenly, we experienced a new and wonderful feeling as if a great weight had been lifted from our shoulders. We were free from all of those denials, discourtesies and restrictions because of our color. We would be accepted at a fine hotel or restaurant: we would be treated like everyone else, with respect. We could enjoy any attractions which were available to other tourists.

I had not realized how imprisoned I had always felt because I was taught to ignore such feelings whenever possible and to rise above them. But at the moment of crossing into Mexico, I felt this new sense of relief, of freedom. Our comment, "Isn't it a terrible shame that we had to leave our own country, our native land, to experience for the first time, a complete sense of freedom as an individual?" But we basked in the experience. We stayed in Mexico ten weeks and returned for at least a month for many years.

Promotion to administrative positions reduced our vacation time to four weeks but fortunately, largely due to the Civil Rights movement, conditions in our country changed somewhat for the better.

A Call From Japan

I often hear from former Phillips High School students. Some have come to see me in Florida and so have some teachers and principals. Some of my rewarding career stories come from the period after my retirement from the Chicago school system. For example, one morning I answered the telephone to find that the call was coming from Japan. It was February 13, my birthday, and the call was to wish me happiness. The call was from a former student at Eckerd College for whom I had served as tutor to help improve her English. She had come, like many foreign students, to engage in conversation and to learn our many idioms. Some stayed for the summer session only, but many remained for a longer period.

This young lady stayed several months; she was interested in two other things beside English. Her uncle in Japan was the owner of a kindergarten and a nursing home where she would be employed some day. She enrolled at Eckerd College, but also served as a volunteer at a local kindergarten and also at the skilled nursing center of College Harbor, the facility where I lived. She would come to my home for our sessions, which were a delight to both of us, and often covered two hours or more at least three or four times each week. Since her return to Japan, she works in the kindergarten. We write and she has sent me several unique little gifts created by a relative.

Tutoring other students even for shorter periods has provided many enriching experiences and I worked with students from Germany, France, Indonesia, Brazil, and elsewhere over a period of seven or eight years. Two young men from Jakarta and a girl from Saudi Arabia became almost a part of our family. She called me her "American mother."

Ladies From Caracas

     One day the receptionist at College Harbor called me to say that there were two ladies at the front desk and she thought perhaps I could be of help to them. I agreed to go down and meet them. The ladies were from Venezuela and had come to St. Petersburg so that their children could attend the summer day camp at Eckerd College. They wanted the children to advance in their English language knowledge and usage. Incidentally, I learned later, when I met the children that they already understood and spoke English quite well. On this day, having enrolled the children, the two ladies left the college for their hotel. When leaving the campus, they noticed buildings in a nearby complex with a huge sign that said, "College Harbor." They decided to go in and find out if there was some kind of program in which they could "bolster up" their own English skills. The receptionist at the front desk explained that College Harbor was a retirement facility, but that some of the residents did sometimes serve as volunteer assistants to college professors or tutored students. The ladies were eager to fill their time practicing English while the children were in day camp. The receptionist thought I might be willing to help and she was correct. We decided after a few minutes of introduction that this project might be fun as well as a learning experience for them and for me. Our travels had not taken Bob and me to South America and we knew very little about Venezuela. We planned to try it out for a few days and then determine if we should continue. Though I protested, they insisted on paying me, so we agreed to wait until we had to terminate our sessions and we could see what it had been worth.

They arrived at my apartment the next day and there we began a most delightful and rewarding teaching experience. I really had no formal method of procedure and I had learned that they really didn't want formal class sessions, so we began by letting each one tell me in English about their homes, families, city, activities, children and husbands' occupations. I took notes of all of the errors in grammar, vocabulary, sentence structure, etc., and from my list, I selected some of the most misused words and we discussed their meaning and use. For homework, they were asked to write sentences using these words. They were pleased and came the next day proudly presenting their completed assignments.

It was because we enjoyed our sessions so much that we met several times each week. It was surprising, for example, how much grammar and facility with the language was derived by playing a simple card game. Examples, "Who dealt?" "Whose deal is it?" "It's your turn." (A new meaning for the word "turn"). "What is the score?" "What is the object of the game?" We talked a lot because they wanted to be better able to converse, but I added some written assignments also. They brought the children to meet me and my husband, and we found them also delightful. When it was time to leave for their home in Caracas, they brought parting gifts: lovely jewelry, and a lovely tall ceramic figurine which had been made in Venezuela by a well-known artist. Then, as they left, one of them pressed an envelope into my hand. When I opened it, there was a note of thanks and a check for two hundred dollars.

Leave Your Glasses Here

The next summer, because of some family business, only one lady returned with her son and daughter (ages about 10 and 11). I received another smaller but somewhat similar figurine. We met less often, but continued our "lessons" and conversations throughout the summer, and a beautiful thing happened when they were ready to leave St. Petersburg.

They had come, mother and children, to say good-bye and we had spent a pleasant evening together. The next evening, the receptionist rang to say those guests were here again. Of course, I welcomed them warmly, but wondered about the visit. I soon learned that the mother thought she had left her prescription sunglasses at our home. Surprised, we began to look for them and yes, there they were on the coffee table unnoticed by Bob or me.

After a short visit, as they approached the open door to leave, the little girl, pointing to a narrow table near the door, said, "Mom, leave your glasses here." Her demure smile indicated her message that then they would have to come back again. Needless to say, I was flattered and happy at the message that her clever remark gave to us.

Different Cultures

Something in my teaching experience that has greatly enriched my life has been the opportunity to teach and work with people from a variety of backgrounds and cultures. As a child in Indianapolis, our elementary schools were racially segregated and so was our social life. Fortunately, in Chicago, my first teaching experience was in a school where the childrens' parents had come to the United States from Italy, Greece and Poland. The faculty had a mixture of races, religions and national backgrounds. In later years, when my husband and I were free and able to travel, we broadened this contact of various cultures, but our earlier experiences enabled us to be at ease and have greater enjoyment than a narrower life would have made possible.

At that first school, Washington Elementary, where I taught for 22 years, my first friend was Jewish and I learned to appreciate some elements of that culture, including some delicious foods, new to me at that time. Occasional invitations to the homes of some of the children and local and somewhat famous nearby restaurants (from which we often ordered lunch) opened to me a new culinary field in Italian foods. Daily association with teachers from everywhere made me a wiser, more open person, better informed and appreciative.

Travel: Cultural Differences

Teaching as a career gave me time to travel and see some of the places about which we had studied and to make them perhaps more real to our students. It was my good fortune to have the opportunity to go to Puerto Rico at a time when we were receiving many pupils from there, and many of us teaching in Chicago needed a better understanding of the culture and customs of Puerto Rico.

As an example, a child in Puerto Rico was taught to cast his eyes downward when being chastised. The American teacher might misunderstand and say, "Look at me when I am talking to you," not realizing that such behavior would have been considered insolent or defiant back in Puerto Rico. Such cultural customs could create problems for both the child and the teacher and acknowledgement of these differences could make the classroom more productive.

Teaching Techniques

Games

I always enjoyed playing games with my students. I recall how the children learned so quickly from some of the games we played when I first began as a teacher in the primary grades. Our principal had his own method of teaching reading, and this included an emphasis on phonics. In my class, we really enjoyed one where several of the children were given large cards; on each card was printed a single letter of the alphabet. In this game, we were making first three, then four-letter words. A child was selected to stand before the class holding his letter and the group would call out the "sound" of that letter. Then, another child would be chosen to stand, then a third. When the three were told to stand together, a word could be formed, such as "m" and "a" and "d." The children would sound out "mad" several times. But when the letter "e" was selected to join them, the students learned that the "a" changed its "sound" to the "long a" and the "e" had to remain silent. With children changing places, the game could continue with lots of words: can and cane, man and mane, hat and hate, mat and mate, for example. This game was fun and the skill was a real help when the children were reading and having to "sound out" new words independently. A similar game taught what happens when a second vowel stands beside the first one, such as rod and road, hat and heat, mat and meat, for example, with the second vowel usually remaining silent, but making the first vowel use its "long a" instead of its "soft a" sound. These were great fun.

Long Division

In two years at what became the Chicago Teachers College, I obtained the knowledge and skills that enabled me to succeed in teaching my classes. I realized, early in my career, how fortunate I was to have had this preparation. Our eighth grade teacher was given a fourth or fifth grade mathematics class in exchange for having her music class taught by a musically talented teacher.

The eighth grade teacher was trying to teach the children long division and she was greatly frustrated. She had made certain that all of them understood the process and had given them practice exercises but the children couldn't do the problems. She said, "And I gave them easy problems – no divisor over 20." I recognized the trouble: the teacher didn't know that 18 and 19, for example, were more difficult than 81 and 91 would be as divisors. She had, therefore, left out one step in her teaching – what to do when the trial divisor doesn't work. I was so glad to be able to help her and through her a whole class of young pupils.

I Want to Be
In That Number

While I was working for my Ed.D. degree, with motivation as my theme, we used a "corny" but "fun device." We were having a competition for improved grades among homerooms. This contest was to be a measure of student growth and a motivation toward greater effort. Wonderful prizes awaited the homerooms making the most progress, or maintaining top level. The children used an old spiritual as their theme song, "I want to be in that number when the saints go marching in" changed, to "When the homerooms win their prize."

Students became so interested and involved that they really worked and helped each other so their room would have a chance. It was the only time I remember ever overhearing one child ask another if she had her homework assignment finished. I even heard the theme song being hummed here and there. This was a very satisfying experience. Everyone was working hard together toward a common, worthwhile goal.

A Place For Everything

My husband's first teaching assignment was for elementary school shop classes: printing, woodworking, etc. I learned something from him which I was able to use in my classrooms and even at home. From one of the instructors at the Teachers College he adopted a motto: "A place for everything, and everything in its place." This motto was good not only for his students and mine, but for teachers I later supervised and their children.

One of the satisfactions of a teaching career is the awareness that the results of your endeavors may help many individuals whom you never see and may continue for years and years in places you never knew. My husband's college teacher and his motto are examples of this.

Creativity

Many teachers during my working years impressed me as being very creative. When books were no longer useful in the classroom, perhaps being replaced by a new edition, schools sent them to a general storage location where they were disposed of, (I'm not sure how.) One teacher, I remember, secured permission to visit that facility and select anything she could use. I believe she had a classroom of third grade students who were poor financially, did not live near a library and had few, if any, books at home.

I was surprised when I visited her classroom as District Superintendent and found books lined up against the chalkboards all around the room (on the three sides without windows). They made an interesting, colorful border and did not interfere with children using the "blackboards" because there was ample space above for writing or solving arithmetic problems.

The teacher and her pupils had set up a library system. Different children had assignments as "clerks" to "charge books out" at 3:15 p.m. each day and receive those being returned each morning. Children selected their own books to take home and also were permitted to quietly choose a book to read in the classroom as soon as they had finished an assignment and before the teacher introduced a new activity. A note to parents had requested and apparently secured their cooperation in seeing that books were returned and hopefully in sharing some of the joy of reading the books with their children. So much benefit from castoff books and a creative teacher! I wonder if that might happen now.

Benefits Of Teaching

Free Time

One advantage which teaching gave us was the opportunity to have a long vacation period in which we could travel. In Chicago, we were paid for the ten months we worked and had to learn to budget our income carefully. For many summers, we spent a few weeks in Mears, Michigan, at the "resort and cherry farm" of two of Bob's former teachers, the Duncans' from Evansville, and later from Gary, Indiana. Other guests were from various cities but all were either friends of the Duncan's or friends of their friends. It was always an interesting group, but what made it so valuable to us was that we found ourselves "recharged" for the work of the next school year.

There were plenty of activities: swimming in Crystal Lake, climbing in a jeep over the sand dunes, enjoying together the bountiful meals and socializing together. It was the wonderful experience, however, of having time when we had nothing which we must do. At home there were always several things awaiting our attention, but at Val-Du-Lakes, we had the choice of activities or of doing nothing. We were free from pressure and it made those weeks delightful and seemed to prepare us for the busy weeks and months ahead.

P.E.L.

Rewards have very often come to me from my involvement with the P.E.L. program at Eckerd College. The Program for Experienced Learners enrolls mature students (none less than 25 years of age) who wish to earn a degree for various reasons. Some want to improve to be more effective in their present positions, some wish to be eligible for promotion, others wish to change careers, and some come for the joy of learning and to enrich their own lives and those of their families, friends and associates.

For a number of years, various professors have invited Bob and me to assist with a P.E.L. class. (Eckerd College called us Resource Colleagues). We have met with classes in U.S. History when they were studying the period of slavery and reconstruction or the period of the "Great Depression" (1929-1934). Other very interesting classes were "Human Development," "Managing Cultural Diversity," and most frequently, "Living, Learning and Vocations," a required course and my favorite.

With the professor present, I would take over the class for a couple of hours, leading discussion, eliciting their input concerning the reading assignments, and sharing my opinions and experiences in relation to the course content. They were interested in the practical aspects and the personal experiences from someone who had lived through the events and conditions about which they had read. I raised questions for them and their questions to me were thoughtful and sometimes very challenging. I had to explain and describe pertinent experiences clearly and explicitly to a group of serious learners. To me, as a teacher, this was always a rewarding evening.

To add to my pleasure, one group invited me to their "farewell" dinner and I have received many letters of thanks from various students and sometimes the professors, also. Recently, since I am getting older, one professors' husband has come for me with a wheelchair in his car, making it unnecessary for me to walk the long distance from the parking lot to the assigned classroom. (College campuses are designed for young people). Another professor arranged for her classes, which I share, to meet in the conference room of the building where I reside.

Rewards

Stories about former students, which come back to us as "Success Stories," bring great joy to a teacher. I am delighted with some of the positions and contributions they have made and are making. Looking over a list of Phillips High School alumni donors to a fundraising effort to give scholarships, I was pleasantly surprised at the number of professional degrees.

It also has been a source of pride that I had a part in the professional growth of mature students at Eckerd College and of school administrators at Nova University. Teachers and others who have continued their education and say it was partially at least due to my efforts or example, provide great satisfaction.

Graduation!

An event which gave all of us great satisfaction was our high school graduation program. This was always a beautiful evening, leaving graduates, parents, and teachers on "cloud nine." This eventful evening did not happen without special preparation and restrictions. No infants were allowed; provisions were made for their care and supervision in our Social Room. No flowers could be presented, and no photographs could be taken until the end of the program. There was, therefore, no confusion, no interruption, only a dignified, elegant performance.

With our splendid band in the pit before the stage and our superior choir seated at the rear of the stage, the senior class sponsor stood, the band played, and the students, clad in caps and gowns, marched in two columns – one on each side of the auditorium. There was brief applause as they took their seats. They were a proud and happy group.

I led one line and our guest speaker led the other. What a joy it was when, on one occasion, my husband was that guest speaker. Later on, when he was principal of the school, one evening it was reversed: I was the guest speaker with each of us leading one line of graduates.

Administrative Support: Authority

During the administrative period of my career, I had the authority to use my training, experience and procedures about solving problems. Extreme measures were rarely necessary simply because I did have the authority to act and this fact was known by all. Of course, misuse of that authority would not have been tolerated. The related circumstance was that I felt I had the full support of my superiors. I tried to pass that feeling of comfort along to my faculty by giving them full support for their positive efforts to help our children, parents and school.

Wouldn't you like to have a website set up so that all your former students could let you know where they are and what they are doing?

Teaching Issues

I Will Go To My Alderman

Parents generally react positively when they are convinced that you are a partner with them in wanting the best for their child. An exception was an incident when I was new as an elementary school principal. A parent, who visited me at school was quite perturbed by something pertaining to her son, perhaps a mild disciplinary action of some kind. I tried to explain our position, but she was still dissatisfied and said, "Well, I guess I'll just have to go to my alderman about this." I understood why she would think this a proper procedure since our schools for more than 12 years had been controlled by political figures and had just, in 1947 - 48, been able to re-establish truly professional administration of the schools. So, confident of the fairness of disciplinary procedure and secure in the freedom from political control and favoritism, I was able to calmly reply, "Well, yes, you do that. Invite him to visit us. But, I should let you know that he did not secure this position for me – I earned it, and he cannot remove me; but I will be happy to talk with him. Please come again when there is a problem; as I said before, you may rest assured that we will only do what we believe is best for your little boy. Thanks for coming."

You Can Change The World

One of the college teachers gave me a thought which I could later share with other students. On her blackboard in front of the room was printed these words, "You can change the world," and written below, "And when you leave this class, you will be expected to do so." The first reaction of some people is, "Me? I am only one person; how can I change the world?"

It was a rewarding experience to spend some time exploring this idea. We discovered cases as examples: the one woman who started our celebration of Mothers' Day and the one woman who started Mothers Against Drunken Driving (whom I met as a member of one of our P.E.L. classes). Closer to home, we were made more conscious of how our words and actions inform or influence others who do the same, consciously or unconsciously, for many others and so on and on. This led back to an emphasis in our reading concerning role models and a discussion of our responsibility as role models. This was an inspirational experience for all of us.

Transfer Policy

I was very fortunate in the quality of teachers and teaching at Willard Elementary, where I stayed two years, and at Phillips High where I was principal for ten years. One problem was the teacher transfer policy. After one semester, a newly assigned teacher could put her or his name on the transfer list seeking placement at another (selected) school. At the end of the year, if approved by the principal of the selected school, the teacher could be transferred to fill a vacancy there.

This ruling had some good and some bad effects. Not many of the teachers lived in the neighborhood of my school, located in what had once been the neighborhood of the elite, but by this time had become the home of several low-cost housing projects. The new teachers were often eager to be transferred to schools near their homes. Of course, I encouraged those who showed promise of being great teachers to stay with us.

This policy had some negative effects on the school they left. It meant that the principal was getting new inexperienced teachers every year. Every endeavor was made to train each new teacher but as soon as she was well adjusted (she or he) might be gone and the principal (and older teachers) would have to start all over. This made it hard to assure that our inner city schools were provided with instruction equal to that in more economically favored locations.

Quality

Many of our teachers became involved with their students' learning and success. They identified with the students and the school, and had no desire to leave even if it meant traveling longer distances. These were dedicated teachers and the students respected and appreciated them. When I came to Phillips as principal, I found a large, excellent faculty some of whom had been there for many years and were wholly devoted to the task of teaching "their children."

Failing Grades

One day, I saw a group of students (four or five) gathered in the corridor. Since this was not permitted, I went to investigate. They were so upset that even my arrival did not stop their chatter. I thought I heard one voice threaten someone and a murmur of approval followed. I was surprised because all of the students were "A" students, juniors and seniors, members of the Honor Society and fine young people, school leaders. I knew them well. Answers to my questions revealed that they had just received their report cards for the first marking period and all had received failing grades. They were shocked and very, very angry. I was able, after a talk with them and assurances that I would immediately investigate, to restore order and secure their pledge to take no action until I could meet with them later in the day in my office.

I discovered that this teacher, a very brilliant scholar in his field, had become angry with the class for some reason and had given all of them, the whole class, failing grades. Those four or five students, who had never received a failing grade, had reacted at once, almost violently. I also discovered that this teacher had just recently moved a cot into his "cloak room" so he would be able to relax there while the students were performing the assigned class experiments. He was totally unsatisfactory in my judgment.

I do not believe that a principal should arbitrarily change grades given by a teacher or require a teacher to do so, under normal circumstances, but this was an unbelievable situation. After a conference and a re-evaluation, new grades were given and recorded. It was the system when a principal gives a teacher a mark of unsatisfactory, for the two of them to have a conference with the Assistant Superintendent of Schools. This was done amicably and the teacher was removed from our school.

Substitute Teaching

For the first year after graduation from Chicago Teachers College (Normal School), I was sent from school to school as needed. That year was better than another college course. I saw how really good teachers organized their classes, motivated their students, and presented parts of the curriculum. I also learned something one should avoid, as I tried, that is, to fill in for a weak or inept instructor. The two weeks I spent substituting in the evening school where the students were adults was a revelation and a joy. These pupils were serious about learning, some trying to complete elementary grades, others in high school. They thanked me for correcting errors of speech or in the papers they presented. I felt well rewarded for the time and effort I gave to teaching those classes.

SCR

One program of which I was a part was also a learning and rewarding experience for me. For three years this experimental program was funded by the government, and it was highly successful in many ways. Briefly, a parent was selected from each of the participating schools in a financially underprivileged area. These parents became members of the faculty and were employed so they could leave the welfare rolls. Members of my staff in the Department of Human Relations were responsible for training them during their first summer of employment. Their job was to bring the home and school together: their title, "School Community Representative." They learned which agencies in the community and in the city could help parents with their problems. They brought parents into the school in small groups to learn what the school was trying to do in various subject areas; they interpreted the homes (values, customs, etc.) to their fellow faculty members. They visited homes, took parents on some of the trips their children took.

The benefits were many and almost immediate. The children and neighbors of these SCR's had a new pride. The SCR's had a dignified helper role, earned community respect, and developed a new self-respect. On the last training day, when certificates were presented with

their families in attendance, those women walking proudly up to receive their certificates were totally different from
the discouraged, hopeless ladies who came on that first day
for training.

This was a terrific lesson. Give people jobs which
pay a living wage, give them training so they can succeed
in those jobs, give them status and respect, give them hope
for a better future and you will see a change in each person and in her (or his) children; perhaps even in the
neighbors, as they see that there is some hope, maybe even
for them.

After three years, the government would no longer
fund the "experimental program" regardless of its success
and value. Many principals, faced with budget problems,
chose to cut elsewhere so they could include their SCR
program as a permanent feature of their schools.

Parents Need Help

Many parents, really desirous of giving their children training and experiences that would enable them to have a good life, actually need help. Unfortunately, in our school curriculum, we fail to provide courses in the important "career" of being a parent. In the Department of Human Relations, we found our staff being called upon to assist parents. In particular, when local School Councils were asked to select a principal from three who were eligible for appointment to their school, our department received a number of calls for advice and was able to suggest criteria, which helped council members to make a reasonable choice.

Parental Discipline

Another way in which we could be of help was related to parental discipline. In too many cases, parents themselves were reared in homes where the only way in which they were punished was by whipping or beating. Therefore, that is what they used, with best intentions, to correct their own children. We could suggest other means so that their children would not grow up believing that the best (or only) way to solve such problems was by physical violence.

A mother can spank a little boy of 9, but how would she control him at 19? This question made some parents willing and eager to find better procedures, solutions that could be applied to or used by adults.

Self-Esteem: Confidence

We, as teachers, shared with parents the value of building the child's self-esteem and confidence. "You are important," "You are somebody," and "You can do it," are very important concepts in the development of a motivated, successful student or adult. We emphasized these lessons at Phillips High School and derived great benefit in the behavior of our pupils.

Appendix

Samples from the many rewarding letters received through the years. They are the ultimate "Pay off."

Former High School Students:

"Thank you so much for being a great role model and a positive influence in our lives. I have always envisioned you and your staff as torch bearers who lighted our way and guided us from the darkness of illiteracy into the light of higher education...I really appreciated the education I received at Wendell Phillips High School."

— James Reed

"I only wish students today could experience the "love education" that was applied to your student body. We have all done well and feel that it was because of our past at Wendell Phillips."

— Eileen Bacon Gilmore

"We both have often expressed our good fortune at being alumni...In addition to great teachers, we were guided by great models such as you and Dr. Robert Lewis. We benefited from a loving and caring learning environment where citizenship and academic excellence were the expectation. Frequently we both recall the lessons of life learned at Phillips and use them as a guide in making decisions. We thank you both for your roles and your leadership."

— George and Patricia A. Mitchell

Office Staff:

"Thank you for being such an inspiration. Everyone in my life knows how much you mean to me and the impact you have had on my growth...It's priceless!"

— *"Jackie" Ashton*

Junior Colleague:

"Know that my prayers and heart are with you, my favorite boss lady, who always served as my special role model."

— *Loretta A. Nolan*

Eckerd College Students:

"Dr. Lewis, You were absolutely awesome! I sat spellbound. Then I asked myself 'Why haven't I met Dr. Lewis before now?' Since that class, I have read the articles about you over and over again. I would like to hear more. You have done so much of what I dream of doing. If and whenever possible Dr. Lewis, I would love the opportunity to sit and just listen to you speak. You speak so eloquently. This is something that I want very much to be able to do. Thank you for sharing.

— *Venetta Smith*

"I certainly never fully realized how important good role models were until I met Dr. Virginia Lewis. As long as I live I will always remember the warmth in her hand–the light in her eyes that spoke volumes. Her spirituality, strength of character and intelligence shone through like a beacon of light on a dark, stormy night. She is an individual, who in her time, has succeeded against tremendous odds. She lived through so much history in our country and grew up as a black woman in a white, male-dominated world. Yet, she had the courage to take a stand and make a positive mark in this world. Dr. Lewis is a national treasure and I will always think of her as my hero. She has given me the inspiration and the vision to succeed and is a wonderful role model to follow."

— Theresa Esposito

——That Long Career——

Virginia F. Lewis was born in 1907, the only child of Charles W. and Malinda Meaux Lewis; but she had two loving sisters and a brother from her mother's first marriage.

She graduated from Shortridge High School in 1922 and entered the Chicago Illinois Normal School where, in 1925, she received her teaching certificate. She began her career as a substitute teacher for one year and then was assigned, in 1926, to the Washington Elementary School. There, for ten years, she taught various grades until 1936 when she became the Adjustment Teacher for the school of about 600 students.

In 1929, she married Robert Lewis, also a young teacher. In 1948, after passing a rigid examination, she and her husband were assigned as elementary school principals, Virginia to Willard School and Robert to Drake, then Williams. After two years, in 1950, she was promoted to Principal of Phillips Elementary and Phillips High Schools with a total of more than 4,000 students. She kept the Elementary school for only one year and until 1960, she devoted herself to the High School which she considers to be her most satisfactory career experience.

Meanwhile, by attending evening school, she received a B.S. and an M.A. degree from Northwestern, and Robert received his M.A. With a leave of absence in 1957-58 they both studied at Harvard University and received the D.Ed. degrees in 1960.

Later, in 1960, Virginia was made Superintendent of District 20, and in 1965, an Assistant Superintendent of the Chicago Public Schools. Her husband replaced her as Principal of Phillips High, then served as District Superintendent of District 13 until his retirement in 1968. Virginia retired in 1972, as required at age 65, and became Consultant for the New Century Reading Corp. She also became the Illinois Coordinator of the Doctoral Program for Educational Leaders of Nova University of Ft. Lauderdale, Florida, until 1978, when an automobile accident grounded them both for a year or two.

After moving to St. Petersburg, Florida, in 1987, Virginia and Robert became "Resource Colleagues" at Eckerd College. Robert died in 2001, but Virginia continues to serve in that capacity.